T0210114

SUICIDE SURVIVAL
FINDING YOUR WILL TO LIVE

DEBORAH M. MUELLER

authorHOUSE

AuthorHouse™
1663 Liberty Drive
Bloomington, IN 47403
www.authorhouse.com
Phone: 1 (800) 839-8640

This book is not a substitute for the assessment, diagnosis, and treatment of any mental health disorders. The ideas contained in these chapters are offered as suggestions to help keep individuals from committing suicide. No book can ever replace the value of the one-on-one interaction between an individual and a mental health professional or family physician. If you are struggling with depression, please consult a mental health or medical professional for treatment in your area.

Published by AuthorHouse 01/29/2020

ISBN: 978-1-7283-4558-1 (sc)
ISBN: 978-1-7283-4559-8 (hc)
ISBN: 978-1-7283-4557-4 (e)

Print information available on the last page.

This book is printed on acid-free paper.

CONTENTS

Dedication..ix

Acknowledgements xi

Introduction...xiii

Chapter 1   E.R.: It Is A Matter Of Life And Death.......................1

Chapter 2   Call The National Suicide Prevention Lifeline 3

Chapter 3   Depression Is Treatable 5

Chapter 4   Medical Exam 7

Chapter 5   Tell Someone..8

Chapter 6   Counseling.. 10

Chapter 7   I Do Not Want To Fail You 12

Chapter 8   Somebody To Love 14

Chapter 9   Vito 16

Chapter 10 What Are You Thinking? 18

Chapter 11 Biologically Speaking 20

Chapter 12 You Are Not Alone 22

Chapter 13 What Was...Equals What Is...Equals What Will
Be...Wrong! 24

Chapter 14 Just Be 26

Chapter 15 You Are Invited...28

Chapter 16 Sensitive 30

Chapter 17 At The End Of My Rope 32

Chapter 18 Depression Is Not A Weakness 34

Chapter 19 Yeah I Am A Failure 36

Chapter 20 Breathe 38

Chapter 21 Resiliency 40

Chapter 22 Survive 42

Chapter 23 Rubber Band.. 44

Chapter 24	Tsunami	45
Chapter 25	Remove Deadly Risk Factors	47
Chapter 26	Trying Too Hard To Be Perfect	49
Chapter 27	The Maybe Game	51
Chapter 28	Drugs And Depression	54
Chapter 29	Control What You Can Control	56
Chapter 30	Life Is About Making Good Decisions	58
Chapter 31	The Small Voice	60
Chapter 32	Stop The Rehearsal	61
Chapter 33	Turn Off The Television	63
Chapter 34	Favorite Books	65
Chapter 35	Vision Board	69
Chapter 36	Take A Hike	71
Chapter 37	Be Your Own Good Company	73
Chapter 38	Cry	75
Chapter 39	Hold Your Pillow	77
Chapter 40	Turn On Lights	78
Chapter 41	Join A Group	80
Chapter 42	Live Performance	82
Chapter 43	Rubber Duckie	84
Chapter 44	Write A Letter	85
Chapter 45	Declutter	87
Chapter 46	100 Activities	89
Chapter 47	Don't Worry	93
Chapter 48	Relationships	95
Chapter 49	Love Your Toes	97
Chapter 50	The "No" Button	99
Chapter 51	Do Not Assume	101
Chapter 52	You Matter	103
Chapter 53	Save A Life	105
Chapter 54	The Other Person	107
Chapter 55	Pretend	109
Chapter 56	100 Words	111
Chapter 57	Create	115
Chapter 58	Should	117
Chapter 59	Nature's Counsel	119

Chapter 60   Shadow.. 121

Chapter 61   No One Lives Forever 122

Chapter 62   A Call For Help.. 123

Chapter 63   Love Letters... 125

Chapter 64   From Duckling To Swan 127

Chapter 65   Attention Is A Powerful Force................. 129

Chapter 66   My Friend Erin 131

Chapter 67   Childhood Wonder 133

Chapter 68   Music 135

Chapter 69   Journal... 137

Chapter 70   Move 139

Chapter 71   Go Play 141

Chapter 72   Gently Down The Stream 143

Chapter 73   Underwhelmed...145

Chapter 74   Lower Your Expectations 146

Chapter 75   Difficult People 148

Chapter 76   The Past 150

Chapter 77   Anger 152

Chapter 78   Death 154

Chapter 79   Be Afraid... 156

Chapter 80   Solutions... 158

Chapter 81   Forgive Yourself 160

Chapter 82   Play For Fun 162

Chapter 83   Laughter 164

Chapter 84   Good Enough... 166

Chapter 85   The Seduction Of Suicide 168

Chapter 86   Your Environment 170

Chapter 87   You Are A Treasure...................................172

Chapter 88   Labels 174

Chapter 89   Self-Nurturer...176

Chapter 90   Haters...178

Chapter 91   Grief.. 180

Chapter 92   Life After Suicide 182

Chapter 93   Martyrdom... 184

Chapter 94   Random Acts Of Kindness....................... 186

Chapter 95   Rooting For You....................................... 187

Chapter 96   Hope 189

Chapter 97   Dream 191

Chapter 98   A Few Extras.. 193

Chapter 99   What Will Keep You Alive?.................... 195

Chapter 100   Final Thoughts.. 197

References... 199

About The Author 209

DEDICATION

This book is dedicated to you if you are struggling with depression. My heart is with you as you seek to find your will to live. I wish you love, purpose, peace, and contentment. Please live!

ACKNOWLEDGEMENTS

I wish to thank my husband and true soulmate in this world, Andrew Mueller. Andy spent hours absorbing and analyzing every word written in this book in an effort to make this book the best the two of us have to offer.

I wish to thank my kindhearted sister, Barbara Burant. Barb read the first draft of this book with love and care. Her devotion to the editing process significantly improved this book prior to its publication.

I wish to thank my dear friend Janet Thulin. Janet sent me newspaper articles and brought my attention to television shows featuring suicide prevention. Her thoughtfulness encouraged me to keep moving forward on this important project.

I love and appreciate each one of you so much!

INTRODUCTION

The first rule of writing is to write what you know. I know about the urge to want to kill myself as I lived with depression day after day, for years, and I have the scars to prove it. I lived in that dark place where hope did not exist, believing that eventually I would die by my own hands. The most important part of my story is that I found a way out of the darkness to a place that is so amazing, a life I would never have believed possible. If you find yourself in a dark place where this idea of self-destruction sounds all too common and you are experiencing thoughts of wanting to commit suicide, I want to offer you 100 options to finding your will to live and thus saving your life. This book was written for you! You can read the book straight through or choose the chapter titles that spark your interest, but whatever you do, keep reading.

The goal of this book and all the energy that went into creating it, is to stop your death from suicide by providing other options for you. If you are determined to kill yourself, there is not much anyone can do to stop you. I understand that. However, if you are in doubt about following through on your plan, please I beg you with every cell of my being to consider other options. I cannot take away your opportunity to end your life because it is not within my power to do so but I can put up roadblocks between that plan, and following through on that plan, by providing avenues to hope. With hope there is life.

Your focus from now on is to stay alive. That's it. Just stay alive. Here are 100 options to help you find your will to live.

Please live!

CHAPTER 1

＋◆◆◆◆＋

E.R.: IT IS A MATTER OF LIFE AND DEATH

As a Licensed Professional Counselor by trade, I had to send suicidal clients to the Emergency Room for help they desperately needed in that moment of their lives. Going to an Emergency Room is not a pleasant experience but the alternative of living with suicidal thoughts and making plans to carry out those thoughts is so much worse.

Once there, you will be assessed. These questions will be about how you are currently feeling. Are you having thoughts of hurting yourself? Do you have a specific plan to take your life? How long have you been feeling this way? Have you ever attempted suicide in the past? Do you currently have the means to follow through on such a plan? By means, they are asking if you have access to the tools to end your life. These questions are asked to see if you need outpatient or inpatient care.

Outpatient care may consist of being prescribed medication to help increase mood transmitters in your brain that make you feel better, while you are coping with the problems that brought on your depression and pain. Medication is frequently paired with counseling because studies show depressive symptoms decrease sooner with the combination of mediation and counseling paired together.

Inpatient hospitalization can seem frightening at first but it is just a place to keep you safe from yourself until you can manage your depressive symptoms and no longer consider acting on your suicidal thoughts. Treatment normally consists of medication and intensive counseling.

In counseling with the psychiatrist, nursing staff, and occupational therapist, you will be given resources specifically designed to help you eliminate your depression. Relieving your depressive symptoms, especially your depressed mood and suicidal thoughts is their goal. They will fight your depression with every resource available because you matter to them.

As unfamiliar and frightening as the thought of going to the Emergency Room may seem, if you are feeling like acting on your suicidal impulses, go directly to the Emergency Room and tell them exactly how you are feeling. They can help because the great news is suicide is preventable because depression is treatable.

Wanting to act on your suicidal thoughts is an emergency. Please go to the Emergency Room and let them do what they do best. Your life depends on you making the right decision in this moment.

Please live!

CHAPTER 2

$\diamond \, \diamond \, \blacklozenge \, \blacklozenge \, \blacklozenge \, \diamond \, \diamond$

CALL THE NATIONAL SUICIDE PREVENTION LIFELINE

Call the National Suicide Prevention Lifeline and connect with people who are trained and truly understand the depth of despair you are feeling. These people actually care about you. They are on the other end of this phone call because your life matters to them.

The people who work on suicide prevention lifelines are committed to keeping you safe and giving you an opportunity to share your pain with them. In this communication, their only goal is to decrease the pain you feel and keep you safe from self-harm. This is what they have committed their lives to. With all their heart and soul, they are talking to you hoping you will find the peace of mind that helps you live longer. They may even have been where you are today and that is their reason for wanting to be in this moment with you now, to save your life.

They understand pain and are trained to listen. Why not give them a chance? What do you stand to lose if you do not call? Everything! What do you stand to gain if you call? Your life! Give them a call, they are waiting to hear from you.

The suicide prevention lifeline is there for you. Give these people a chance to make a difference in your life. You will most definitely make a difference in their life! Isn't that what life is really all about, connecting and helping each other?

Here are the phone numbers. Please call right now if you need to talk to someone who cares about you.

Please live!

NATIONAL SUICIDE PREVENTION LIFELINE
1–800–273–8255
1–800–273–(TALK)
CRISIS SUPPORT IN SPANISH CALL 1–888–628–9454

CHAPTER 3

DEPRESSION IS TREATABLE

You do not have to live with depression. This is one of the most important messages in this entire book. You do not have to live the rest of your days in despair. You do not have to live with hopelessness like a cloud that follows you wherever you go, and whatever you do, you cannot seem to get out from under it.

Depression has a set of symptoms, the same as physical diseases have a set symptoms; such as depressed mood, weight changes, sleep difficulties, psychomotor agitation, fatigue, loss of energy, diminished ability to concentrate, feelings of worthlessness, excessive guilt, and suicidality. Treatment for depression works to eliminate these symptoms so you can live without them.

Treatment for depression will address all of these symptoms, and you will know when the treatment for your depression is working because you will be more focused on living than on dying. You will have a normal appetite, sleep better, feel more relaxed, have more energy, concentrate better, have a sense of worth, and most importantly no longer feel like suicide is even an option for you to consider. This is what I want for you. This is why I am urging you, and I will keep urging you throughout this book to get treatment. Let a family physician, psychiatrist, or ER doctor treat the symptoms of your depression so you feel better. That is why these professionals chose the career they did in order to be here in this moment with you.

If you fell and broke your arm or leg, you would not expect yourself to live with those broken bones and all the pain associated with it for the rest of your life. You would seek treatment and allow a surgeon to repair your broken bones. Seeking treatment for depression is no different, allow a doctor to treat your depression so you do not have to live with pain for the rest of your life.

Imagine waking up rested with plenty of energy to start your day. Imagine being happy to get out of bed and feeling good about yourself and your ability to handle whatever comes along. Imagine being excited about living life. Once your depression is treated, you don't have to just imagine that, you will be able to live that way every day.

For your wellbeing, the best outcome for treating your depression is a combination of medication and counseling. Do both. Ask your doctor for a referral for a mental health professional. You do not have to live with symptoms of depression, not in this day and age. Depression is treatable so please get the treatment you deserve so you can live depression free.

Please live!

CHAPTER 4

✦✦✦✦✦

MEDICAL EXAM

Please see your doctor for a complete medical exam. If you are experiencing problems with mood, appetite, energy, or sleep, this may be an indication you could be clinically depressed. The great news is that depression is treatable.

Did you know these same symptoms could be caused by a problem with your thyroid? Changes in mood, appetite, energy, weight, and sleep may also indicate a thyroid condition that mimics depressive symptoms. This is why it is vital to know the correct diagnosis in order to receive the correct treatment. Again, the great news is that thyroid conditions are treatable.

Whether you have depression or a thyroid issue, you can rest assured help is available from your family doctor. The only way to know for sure why you are experiencing these symptoms is to schedule an appointment with your doctor and go in for a complete medical exam. Tell your doctor about all of the symptoms you are experiencing and when they started. Please, take good care of yourself by making an appointment as soon as you can. This is important because you matter.

Please live!

CHAPTER 5

❖ ✦ ✦ ✦ ✦ ✦ ❖

TELL SOMEONE

Tell someone you are feeling depressed and considering ending your life. I know this may not be easy, but it is important you receive the support you need at this time in your life.

You may have tried many other ways to handle your depression on your own, however there comes a time when you have to reach outside yourself to let someone else know you are in pain. Let me be clear. Be completely honest with someone that you are considering ending your life, whether that person is your family physician, parent, spouse, partner, adult child, sibling, friend, boss, co-worker, teacher, or clergy.

If you commit suicide the people in your life will know you were experiencing a significant life event issue and you did not ask them for help. Better to let people know ahead of time and give them a chance to make a difference in your life. How many people have the opportunity to be a "hero?" You are giving these people a chance to do something good in their lifetime by saving you. Let them do this for you because you both deserve happiness.

If the person you tell gets it wrong, maybe by not knowing what to say; or worse yet, saying something hurtful to you that makes your situation worse, tell someone else. Keep telling someone until you receive the acknowledgement and support you need to live a full and happy life.

Right now as you read these words, do you know you deserve to feel better? Do you know that a life without depression and despair is possible? All you have to do to begin the process to a happier and more enriched life is to find the right person to tell; a person who will be so thankful to have the opportunity to help you, and most importantly, to see you survive.

Please tell someone today.

Please live!

CHAPTER 6

✦ ✦◆✦◆✦ ✦

COUNSELING

Counseling is a must. If you are depressed, the good news is you do not have to continue suffering. Can you even imagine a life without gut-wrenching suffering? Counseling with the right counselor, for you, can alleviate your suffering.

Over the years, I went from being a client diagnosed with Major Depression to a Licensed Professional Counselor in order to help other individuals who suffered from mental and emotional disorders. During my first marriage, I was treated by nine different mental health professionals. I sought counseling from time to time for the major depression that kept recurring. Each counselor was different, some were better than others for me. Interestingly, the final counselor, Dr. Cruikshanks, was the one I could relate to the best and I had a complete awakening under his care and guidance. I went from a place of hating myself to a place where I learned to love myself. As this occurred, I could no longer stay in the unhealthy relationship with my husband, and we divorced which was a pivotal turning point in my life. Once I realized how valuable my life was, I was no longer able to accept any relationship that did not honor that value.

One reason I could relate to Dr. Cruikshanks was because he shared, early on in a counseling session with me, that he too had been clinically depressed at an earlier time in his life. He knew firsthand how it felt to not know if he could make it through a day without giving in to the depression and ending his life. He even had a suicide attempt, so he knew what I was feeling and thinking. Most importantly, he knew there was a way out of the depression and that life could get better. He knew it for himself and he knew it for me. In a way, he plotted a course for me out of the "woods of depression" as he called it. I often strayed off that path and would spiral down. I did not give up, and as time passed, I continued my journey to a better place; I felt better about myself, my future, and life overall. My thoughts became more positive and life became worth living. Later, I would chronicle that path in my first book *Sadistic Love: My Twenty-Two Year Marriage To A Sexual Sadist*. As counseling with Dr. Cruikshanks came to an end, I thanked him for everything he had done to change my life, and he pointed out I had done the work to make the changes possible. Dr. Cruikshanks had given me the sight and direction to do so. This is why counseling is so important.

I was so intrigued with the process of counseling that I went on to receive my Master of Arts in Counseling Degree. As a Licensed Professional Counselor, I witnessed the healing power of counseling. Often, clients came to their first appointment anxious about how the counseling process would work. Both men and women would come into counseling, and after a bond of trust was formed, they would let down their guard and speak of the unspoken in their lives. Time and time again lives were changed because the process of being truly heard and understood in counseling made a profound difference in their lives.

I am counseling's biggest fan. The right counselor can take you from the depth of depression to a place where you can survive and even flourish. Please seek help from a mental health professional because counseling can truly be life-saving for you.

To find a mental health professional in your area go to www. psychologytoday.com and enter your city or zip code in the "Find a Therapist" box on their website; or contact your family doctor for a referral.

Please live!

CHAPTER 7

◆◆◆◆◆◆

I DO NOT WANT TO FAIL YOU

As I sit here in the family room of our home, on the couch with a notebook and pen in hand, I realize the importance of putting the words together for this book. I have taken this task seriously by the amount of time and thought I put forward over this past year because your life matters to me. Trying to think of the right words that will convince you to give life another chance has become my focus and my life.

I want to be the person who comes through for you. I want to be the person who makes you question that committing suicide is not the right choice for you, because if I can get you to question the choice between living or dying, then I hope you will choose to live. I want to widen the gap between thinking about taking your life, and acting on taking your life, as far apart as I can. My goal is that you receive the support you need during this period of doubt. If I can help you choose life at this time then there is hope that we can work together through these pages to save you and offer you a happier life. I do not want to fail you, this is why I have worked so hard to write this book for you.

If in this book, you do not read the words you need to hear to stay alive, then consider writing them for yourself. Feel free to add as many chapters to this book that you need so you have the words that give you comfort in a time of self-doubt. This is the time to do whatever works to keep you alive.

I know at this time, you think you know what the future holds for you because of your experience of the past when in reality, no one knows what the tomorrows, months, and years to come will hold for them. I sat on a much different couch at one time, an old used couch that was donated to me by a family member because I could not even afford to purchase a used one at a thrift store. I could barely afford food for my children during those times. My life today is like nothing I had ever experienced or even imagined possible during those dark times. Your life circumstances will change as well and the choices you make now will determine whether you will have the opportunity to experience these changes in your future.

It is possible to live a life without depression and to get to a place where you are deliriously happy. I know this because I have experienced these changes myself. I had been so depressed in the past, that the idea of leaping off into the image I held of a dark abyss below me, seemed so much more tolerable in that moment than ever having to turn around and face my life circumstances. Now, the sun rises every morning and I am delighted to see it, a far far cry from standing at the edge of that dark abyss wanting to end my life.

Please let me lead you away from your dark abyss and choose life. Please find in these words the help you seek to move far away from the abyss and into a life filled with love, enjoyment, and contentment. Find your way to the core of your being where love and life flourishes.

Do not let me fail you. Keep holding on until you find your way to a better frame of mind, one where depression no longer exists. Life is worth fighting for. Believe me, I would not be saying this if it were not possible. I now live depression free and happy and so can you.

Please live!

CHAPTER 8

❖❖❖❖❖

SOMEBODY TO LOVE

My three children, even though they didn't know it, kept me from ending my life. Dying for my children seemed easy but living for them was much harder because I was in so much emotional pain from the depression. Being their mother kept me alive for them.

A counselor once told me that if I committed suicide, it would destroy my children for the rest of their lives. The counselor said he knew this to be true because of the work he had done in counseling with grieving families. I believed him because I knew how upset I felt about individuals I had known that ended their lives by their own hands and how upset I felt about their lives ending so tragically in that manner. These individuals were not close friends but their deaths disturbed me just the same. This is why I knew what the counselor was saying to be true.

I would never do anything that would hurt my children, in fact I did everything I could think of to shelter them and keep them safe; and to keep my depression hidden from them and everyone else. I could not allow my internal pain to negatively impact my children so I kept fighting the depression by seeking help which required several psychiatric hospital admissions. These hospitalizations along with follow-up counseling, and psychotropic medications kept me alive. Now, I not only survived all those years of darkness, but I live depression free and have not been clinically depressed nor needed psychotropic medication for the past fifteen years. It is so wonderful to wake up every morning and never think about hurting myself ever again.

You need to focus on your somebody to love; your somebody to live for. It can be a child, parent, brother, sister, spouse, partner, grandparent, aunt, uncle, niece, nephew, friend, co-worker, pet; or as far-fetched as this sounds, it can even be me. Even though we have never met in person, you matter to me. You and I have shared a similar type of pain, and I don't want that for you. Pick someone you are willing not to hurt by your death, and keep yourself alive for them.

Suicide is devastating to those left behind. You may be fooling yourself that those who love you will be better off without you, but that is not true, that is your depression talking. That's not the reality they will be experiencing. In truth, you have no real idea what they will be going through without you. Those that you leave behind are tortured by thoughts of "what if?" What if I could have said something or taken some action the last time we were together that would have made the difference? What about our relationship, wasn't my love enough? What did I do wrong that caused this? How can I ever forgive myself? How can I ever forgive them?

Suicide does not end with your death. Your suicide will live in the hearts of all those individuals who have ever known you. If you feel like you can't live for yourself right now, please live for them. You can't go to your own funeral and see the heavy hearts, the total devastation, and the sadness your death causes the people who knew you. You won't be there to comfort them, or worse yet, you could be there 'in spirit' and still not be able to comfort them.

Pick one or two people and focus on not hurting them. The pain your suicide would cause them is preventable, all you have to do is live. Fight your depression one more time and spare them a lifetime of heartbreak and pain. Instead, allow them to become Heroes because they saved your life whether they know it or not. Please live for them.

Please live!

CHAPTER 9

◆◆◆◆◆◆

VITO

Pet lovers, if you have difficulty surviving for your family and friends, then live for your pet. Man's best friend, a dog, cat, bird, fish, or whatever pet you love can provide the support, companionship, and love that is needed in your life. Time spent with a lifelong friend can be invaluable.

I once had a client, Joseph, who came to my office for his scheduled appointment on a day we were babysitting our daughter's new puppy named Vito, a black pug. I put Vito upstairs in his cage for the appointment with Joseph because nothing disturbed my time with my clients. Vito didn't know about this rule and began crying. Joseph heard Vito cry and asked me to please allow him to come down and join us. Reluctantly, I did and Joseph ended up holding Vito for the entire session. What was most amazing and enlightening to me was how Vito calmed and opened Joseph's heart. I learned a valuable lesson about the importance of pet therapy that day. I had previously heard about the value of pet therapy, but had never witnessed this emotional bond until that moment.

When our hour was up, I told Joseph that I should not charge him given that we had this unexpected interruption from Vito. My very wise client told me I should charge him double for providing him with pet therapy. This is the moment he shared that a few days prior to this appointment with me, his dog had to be put to sleep due to old age. Vito gave him an hour worth of comfort and peace.

Pets can be comforting, lift spirits, and so helpful to individuals in need of emotional support; and who among us couldn't use some additional emotional support? Dogs can even be trained as guides. A program like "Wags 4 Warriors" that assist veterans who are dealing with depression, anxiety, or post-traumatic stress disorder by providing them with a dog of their own to care for, speaks to the healing power of pets.

Having a pet, regardless of what type of pet that is, gives you a purpose. They are living souls that require you to show them love and care, and in return, they provide you with years of emotional support, comfort and love. They really do love you.

If you are depressed and need emotional support, consider adopting a pet.

Please live!

CHAPTER 10

WHAT ARE YOU THINKING?

If you are feeling bad, it has everything to do with your thinking. What are you telling yourself? What are your thoughts? Are these thoughts something you would wish for your best friend, or someone you love to be thinking about themselves? If you are having suicidal thoughts then you are in desperate need of changing your thoughts.

If you are saying negative things to yourself, I am here to tell you that you are not telling yourself the truth. It may feel like the truth to you, when in reality it is false. When an individual is depressed it is as though they see everything inaccurately because depression robs an individual of rational thinking.

For instance, when I was depressed, I believed with all my heart that I was not smart. At the time, I was in my early forty's and going back to college to obtain my bachelor degree in psychology. I was doing well in my classes, but held on to the irrational belief from my childhood that I was not one of the intelligent siblings in my family. In reality, I not only earned my undergraduate degree, but I graduated with honors, then went on to earn a Master of Arts in Counseling Degree, and graduated with a nearly perfect G.P.A. (grade point average). The truth, as it turned out, was that I was smart despite doubting my abilities because of seeing the world through my depression.

You may be misled by your thinking as well. You may also believe something about yourself that feels like the truth to you, but in reality is not true. What would the possibilities be if you would see the world without your depression? What would you be able to accomplish without this restriction in your life?

First, you really need to start listening to what you are saying to yourself about yourself. Are your words kind to yourself? Remember the Golden Rule, do unto others as you would have them do unto you? I believe that if you suffer from depression, you need to turn the Golden Rule around by treating yourself as good as you treat those you love. Stop saying negative things to yourself that you would never say to someone else.

Listen to what you are saying to yourself and when you say something negative, change that into something positive that will empower you to recognize your value. Nothing good comes from beating yourself up by saying nasty or mean things to yourself, so stop the bullying inside your head. This is the time to be kind to yourself.

Change your thoughts. Focus on something positive, even something small and seemingly insignificant each and every day. If you begin to search for more positive thoughts, you will feel better about yourself because where your thoughts are, your feelings will follow. Above all remember this, what you are telling yourself matters and will make a huge difference in your life. It all begins with, what are you thinking?

Please live!

CHAPTER 11

BIOLOGICALLY SPEAKING

If you suffer from depression and you feel as though things are not going well in your life, the depression you are experiencing may be caused by a biological imbalance. We all have neurotransmitters in our brains that are responsible for being able to experience pleasure, joy, and happiness. Neurotransmitters are chemicals such as dopamine, serotonin, and norepinephrine. There is so much we are still learning about exactly how neurotransmitters work in the brain.

What we do know is that if your brain is not producing enough of one of these chemicals, or not using these chemicals effectively, it can cause depression. Your brain can be "serotonin-ly" deficient. It is not something you caused to happen, in fact it is no different than a person with diabetes needing to take insulin because of being insulin deficient. If you are clinically depressed, you may need to take an anti-depressant medication in order to help your body increase serotonin, or use serotonin more effectively so you can live without depressive symptoms.

If you and your doctor decide you need to be on anti-depressant medication, do not view this as a failure on your part. Instead see the truth of the situation and know that your body, for some reason, is not producing enough serotonin, dopamine, or norepinephrine; or not using these chemicals effectively. I really hate it when people judge other people and make inaccurate statements such as, "buck up," "pull yourself together," or "quit being so weak." This person would never say this to an individual needing insulin for their diabetes. You need to ignore people like this and do what is best for you. If your doctor prescribes an anti-depressant medication, take it, and keep taking it. I had a friend who shamed me for "having" to take a psychotropic medication because she felt I should be able to handle life without having to take a pill to get through the day. Years later, she experienced depression and was put on the same anti-depressant medication that I was prescribed. She called me to apologize for her opinions years earlier because now she truly understood the benefits of this psychotropic medication.

Psychotropic medications helped to save my life during those depressed years, and because of taking them I am alive today. Depression is treatable, and medication with counseling is your best pathway to survival. According to research, medication combined with counseling is the best option to treat depression and keep the symptoms from reoccurring.

After years of suffering from depression and taking nineteen different psychotropic medications over a twenty-two year span, I have now been depression free for fifteen years. I no longer take any psychotropic medication because the need for this type of medication is gone. If my circumstances change, and I slip back into depression, I will seek counseling and if psychotropic medication is recommended I will not hesitate to begin taking it once again to feel better. I never want to go back into that darkness again. Fortunately I live in an era in history where I do not have to go without professional help and medication to live depression free.

If you are prescribed medication for depression, stay on it. If that medication does not help you feel better, let your doctor know so a different medication can be prescribed, or even several together to find the right combination so ultimately you live depression free, focused, and happy.

Please live!

CHAPTER 12

❖ ✦◆✦◆✦◆✦ ❖

YOU ARE NOT ALONE

Who knew being a superintendent at a golf course could be so stressful it would cause good-hearted, hard-working individuals to beat themselves up so severely they would come to believe suicide was a viable option to ending their pain? An article in Golf Digest written by Ron Whitten, "Silent Struggles Taboos & Tattoos: Superintendents Are Taking Steps To Save Colleagues Who Contemplate Suicide" (October 2019) discusses the depression and anxiety plaguing four brave superintendents who have stepped forward to address their struggles with depression in order to help others.

If you are depressed and have thoughts and feelings about committing suicide, you are not alone. According to an article on www.washingtonpost.com by William Wan, "Once They Hid Their Stories. But Now, Survivors Of Suicide Are 'Coming Out' To Combat A National Crisis" (July 29, 2019), Wan reported that 130 Americans die by suicide every day. In 2017, more than 47,000 Americans died by suicide and 1.4 million attempted suicide. Suicide is the 2nd leading cause of death by teens and young adults.

One person committing suicide is a tragedy. 47,000 people dying by suicide in one year is unimaginable. This does not have to be our reality because suicide is preventable because depression is treatable. Please seek out a mental health professional if you are experiencing anxiety and depression. You do not have to suffer in silence.

Let's start being honest about our struggles. So many of us put on a happy face and go out into the world without ever letting people know what is really going on behind our smile. Let's start talking about how we are really feeling.

That may not seem easy because of the fear that if you let your guard down, there will be individuals who will use your vulnerability to hurt you. For instance, when one superintendent from the above mentioned article in Golf Digest shared his struggle with fellow superintendents, he received "60 emails mostly supportive" because so many could relate to having depression and wanting to kill themselves too.

The superintendent's use of the words "mostly supportive" told me, he also received emails from people who do not understand what individuals go through when they suffer in silence with depression. How sad that there were actually some people who were not supportive. This speaks to the courage these superintendents demonstrated by coming forward and by doing so helped others come forward to seek the treatment they needed as well. When you know you are not the only person with these thoughts and feelings, and you learn about others experiencing relief from depression by seeing a mental health professional for treatment, it makes it easier to do the same. These four superintendents remind me of one of my favorite quotes by Stephanie Sparkles, "I love when people who have been through Hell, walk out of the flames carrying buckets of water for those still consumed by the fire."

Be brave. You are not alone out there. Seek the help that is available to you.

Please live!

CHAPTER 13

✦✦✦✦✦✦✦

WHAT WAS...EQUALS WHAT IS...EQUALS WHAT WILL BE...WRONG!

Yesterday, today, and tomorrow are all different places in time. Depression can make you believe the hopelessness you feel trapped in today, is how you have always felt, and as if there was never a time in your past when you were happy. Worse yet, your depression will make you believe you will always be trapped in this hopeless state of mind, robbing you of any chance at a happier existence. I know how this can feel for you but this is not the reality of the situation. Depression dominates your thinking and makes you believe that how you feel right now is the way you will always feel, but the reality is you have the power to change all the tomorrows to come.

What if tomorrow, whenever that tomorrow comes, is filled with something wonderful which brings you happiness like you have never experienced before? How do you know with one hundred percent certainty this is not the case? What if something so extraordinary is about to happen for you that you have never even dreamed possible? Something so wonderful may be waiting for you just around the corner that you are unable to see quite yet. The truth is, good things happen for all of us. What if your good things are coming tomorrow?

What if you are not here to receive it? This is why you must keep fighting your way through your depression in order to live to receive the good that is coming your way.

For so many years, I lived in what my counselor at the time, Dr. Cruikshanks, called "the woods of depression." I felt alone and lost in those dark woods without the ability to ever go beyond that depressing place. I often wonder why I was able to make it out of those dark woods of depression when so many other depressed individuals could not. It may have been that I finally had just the right combination of forces that came together for me; my three children to love, family to live for, a few supportive friends, a great counselor who helped me to work through my depression and build up my self-worth, and finally the correct psychotropic medications. I overcame my depression and every day I am extremely thankful to be alive and to enjoy my life to the fullest extent possible.

I want the same happiness for you. I am not special. If this transformation from depression to living depressed free happened for me, I know it will happen for you too. How you feel today will be completely different than how you feel tomorrow. Do not allow your negative feelings today to rob you of your happier tomorrows.

Please live!

CHAPTER 14

✦✦✦✦✦✦

JUST BE

Just be. If you are having difficulty and find yourself overwhelmed by the roles you play: mother, father, daughter, son, sister, brother, aunt, uncle, niece, nephew, grandparent, spouse, partner, friend, co-worker, boss, oldest, youngest, etc.; just STOP! You are, essentially, without any of these roles, a human being. Please give yourself permission to just be.

What does it mean to just be? If means stripping away all the roles you strive for perfection to play, and let yourself rest. Give yourself time to pull away from the demands of these roles as much as you possibly can for some quiet time, rest, and peace.

What would happen if you were unburdened by the roles that you play and actually let yourself just be? Would your world come to an end? Given that you are carrying all these roles you have taken on, are you coming to your end under the weight of it all? If you are nearing the end of your endurance to cope with all you are striving to accomplish, then it is time to stop and let go of the roles you play.

Obviously, if children are involved, you cannot and should not abandon your role as a mother or father; however, you could carve out some time in your day for quiet time and rest. The more you rest and rejuvenate, the more energy you will have to give back to your parenting role.

If work is the main stressor then make the changes that are necessary to help you cope with this stress. If that requires you to seek a different position with your present employer or with a different company altogether, then make that happen. Just be aware that if you are stressed and depressed your ability to perform your job is significantly reduced. Make sure you are taking advantage of all your vacation time, family-leave time, and sick days available to you. Do what you need to do to stay alive. No company will fall apart without you, make sure you do not fall apart for the sake of the company and do what you need to do to survive. Just be.

Just be also means you find ways to focus on being alive. You are so much more than your depression. Step off the quick-paced treadmill and find ways to rest and relax.

Just be.

Please live!

CHAPTER 15

◆ ◆ ◆ ◆ ◆

YOU ARE INVITED

Please R.S.V.P. a "Yes!" Your future holds upcoming events, that in your depressed state, you have not been able to focus on. I ask that you spend some time now giving these personal invitations some consideration. There are upcoming events that need your participation so please say "Yes" you will be there for all future events.

The future holds only a place you can fill. There was a little boy named Jason, that I knew, who had plans to visit his Aunt Kathy for Halloween so he could show her his new costume. Unfortunately his Aunt Kathy was not there for Halloween. Kathy had ended her life a few days before they were getting together. His aunt committed suicide even though she was very aware she had these plans with her nephew for Halloween. Sadly, Kathy would never again see her nephew, Jason, or his costume. Her decision not to be there for him left a life changing tear in this young child's life and impacted and darkened the entire Halloween holiday because now his family was having to prepare for her funeral.

This true story is even more tragic when you realize Kathy never had to die because suicide is preventable because depression is treatable. I attended her funeral and it was so heartbreaking because family members and friends did not know she was in such a dire place in her life. Following her funeral, I began to put chapters together to write this book knowing I could no longer reach out to Kathy, but in my sorrow, I could write a book that hopefully would help others choose a different option for themselves.

There are holidays, birthdays, weddings, graduations, picnics, baby showers, retirement parties, weddings, anniversaries, bar mitzvahs, baptisms, and many other events and gatherings that require your presence. Even if those things do not seem important to you at this moment, they are important to your family and friends who will be attending these events. Your absence will be noted and the event will not be the same without you. People need to know they matter to you. Your absence, due to your suicide, makes them feel they can never be completely happy ever again. Even if you don't believe it, you will always be missed.

No matter how much fun you have had or how much fun those around you have had in the past, your absence, if you go through with ending your life will leave a void in all future gatherings. You probably know what it is like to miss a loved one who has died. Missing a loved one who has taken their own life and left sooner than they were supposed to, leaves a sadness that is beyond words. Do not let this happen.

R.S.V.P. "Yes." Say you will be there.

Please live!

CHAPTER 16

SENSITIVE

I have a theory, and I could very well be wrong, but I think it takes a sensitive person to think about committing suicide. Often, I will hear people say that thinking about suicide is so selfish, and with those words, they almost add an additional layer of loathing on top of an individual who is already drowning in self-loathing. It is a harsh judgement that does not have the understanding or the compassion for the depth of emotional pain an individual is experiencing, where suicide seems to be the only way out of their pain.

People who commit suicide are not selfish, they are sensitive souls who have not discovered another way out of their pain. They wear their hearts on their sleeves. Life does matter to them, but it matters too much and becomes too heavy to bear because of everything that has broken their hearts. They do not really want to be dead, they are desperate for a way out of their pain. Wanting to commit suicide is not selfish but rather a misguided thought process that following through on ending their life will somehow be better for them and everyone else.

Years ago, at one of my first counseling sessions when I was the client suffering from postpartum depression, at the same time my husband lost his job, I remember asking the counselor to make me stronger so I would not be so sensitive. He told me that my sensitivity was a gift and not something I had to work to eliminate. He said being sensitive meant I had compassion and empathy for others and he did not want to take that from me. What I needed most was to learn to set boundaries so I did not allow people to take advantage of my compassion. I truly understand that much more now than I ever did back then.

Sensitivity is a gift. What you need to learn is to turn your sensitivity inward toward yourself by stop being so hard on yourself. Turn the compassion you have for others inward and take care of yourself the same way you take care of others. Talk to yourself like you talk to others. Save yourself as you would save others.

My other theory is that 98% of the population consists of sensitive people. The other 2% lost their sensitivity somewhere along the way and only know how to make life painful for themselves and everyone they come across. There are degrees of sensitivity but I believe people are much more sensitive than we realize and this goes for both women and men, young and old, wealthy or poor, spiritual or atheist, gay or straight. Each of us are sensitive but we deal with our sensitivity differently. Boys are taught not to cry, girls are taught not to show anger, so we learn to deal with our sensitivity and often hide what we do not believe we are allowed to express. We are not always authentic on the outside because we have been taught or conditioned to act "appropriately."

Do you find this to be true? When I began counseling, I had a client come in for his first session and I have to admit I was intimidated by his size and manner of dress, he looked like one tough guy. Half way through the session he started to cry, he could not help himself, the tears just flowed out of his eyes. He was in so much pain with no one in his life to share his pain with him. He believed he was not "allowed" to cry but in that moment could not hold his sadness in any longer. My heart went out to him and he felt the compassion and empathy from me. That day he taught me a valuable lesson about my image of sensitive people, and I will forever be grateful to him for that valuable lesson.

Sensitivity is a gift. You are never too sensitive, you only need to be aware of where your sensitivity leads you. Let sensitivity keep your heart open, at the same time you are using your sensitivity to care for yourself.

Please live!

CHAPTER 17

◆◆◆◆◆◆◆◆◆◆

AT THE END OF MY ROPE

When you feel like you have tried everything, and nothing seems to be working the way you believe it should, you may be telling yourself that you are at the end of your rope. This is a common phrase in our society indicating there are no alternatives left; that is it; "it's" over. What if you take that thought of being at the end of your rope and magically extend your imaginary rope out as far as you need it to be?

Holding onto images that are not empowering only continues to harm you. As a society, we do this all the time. When I was at the end of my rope, it never occurred to me to simply make the imaginary rope extend out as far as I needed it to be or better yet, to imagine a more empowering image to help me get through my depressed thoughts. Instead of being "at the end of my rope," with my "back up against a wall," or with "nowhere to run," or "up a creek without a paddle," or "down in the dumps," or even "shit out of luck;" I should have chosen an image that would have empowered me to overcome my sense of helplessness.

We live in the worst case scenario when we hold these destructive images in our thoughts. The image you hold in your thoughts generates the energy you feel. Do you want to feel good? Of course you do because we all want that for ourselves. Holding onto positive images in your mind will produce good feelings for you and the best part is that this is an area of your life you have complete control over, your own imagination.

Feel the energy difference in the following opposing statements:

waiting for the other shoe to drop versus just another day in paradise; being down and out versus being on top of the world; I don't have a pot to piss in versus I am a money magnet. See how your positive thoughts improve your outlook on life by choosing empowering and feel good images. Remember the next time you are at the end of your rope, you do have the power to imagine your restrictive rope magically extending out as far as you need it to be. The rope is only imaginary but your feelings behind the image are real. The hope is that by changing the image, your negative feelings will change to more confident thoughts. This is why choosing a more empowering image brings you to a happier place.

Please live!

CHAPTER 18

DEPRESSION IS NOT
A WEAKNESS

Depression does not care if you are female, male, or transgendered; it does not care if you have a large bank account or none at all; and it does not discriminate on the basis of age, political party, education, race, or religion. Depression can strike at any time in any individual, much like a cancer. The first time I was admitted to a psychiatric ward of a hospital for being suicidal, I remember being surprised that the patient in the next room was a CEO of a thriving company and another patient on the floor was a beautiful young woman. Depression had impacted both of them as well.

You are not experiencing depression because you are weak, you are experiencing depression because you are human. Any individual is susceptible to depression during their lifetime.

Life is complicated. Negative life events you never see coming can hit you so hard and throw you off balance. Things may be going along fairly well when a negative life event comes along and takes you in a direction you never expected you would be dealing with, or could have ever been prepared for.

The sense of being thrown off balance can be traumatic. Death of a loved one, a crippling car accident, a divorce, a miscarriage, losing a job, a significant relationship in turmoil, a natural disaster, and war are some significant life events that can lead to anxiety and despair. People have understandably good reasons for being depressed, something happened to them that triggered the start of their depression.

This is why counseling is so vital. Counseling offers an opportunity to pull back the layers of despair to see what caused the depression to occur. With this understanding, coping mechanisms can be put in place to ease the trauma of the negative experience and lessen the anxiety and depression.

There is a very good reason why you are depressed whether you are aware of the underlying root cause or not. On top of being depressed, do not cause yourself further trauma by beating yourself up for feeling the way you do and thus worsening your situation. Depression is not a personal weakness, rather it is the body's way of telling you something is really wrong and needs your attention. You need to stop and listen to what your body is telling you, but when you do, please listen with compassion. Do not judge yourself harshly, just listen.

If you feel weak, know that when your depression is treated, you will gain your strength back. Depression is a temporary reaction to negative life events. Be kind. Put yourself in an emotional ICU and take care of yourself as best you can during this traumatic time.

Please remember you are not weak, you are human. Do not give up on yourself. You will pull through the trauma to a place where your negative feelings will no longer define who you are. Break free from depression by seeking treatment. Do not suffer alone.

Please live!

CHAPTER 19

✦✦✦✦✦✦

YEAH I AM A FAILURE

I am thankful beyond words to express that I am a failure. I attempted to end my life in 1997 but I failed because I did what was vital in that moment and reached out for the help I needed to save my life.

There have been so many times since my suicide attempt that I have been so thankful I failed at failing. If I had succeeded, I would not have been there to watch my children graduate from high school, college, law school, or get married. I would never have met Andrew Mueller, my true soulmate; and by attempting suicide, I risked never knowing a love like him in my lifetime. I would never have held our first grandchild in my arms when she was only a few hours old, or our second granddaughter, or our first grandson. I would not have spent the week with my brother a few months before he died, a week that was such a gift to both of us. I would have missed birthdays, holidays, weddings, Sisters Week, and our son's hole-in-one on the golf course. I would not have received a Master of Arts in Counseling Degree, opened up my own counseling practice and helped other people through their life challenges, nor published several books. I would have missed all of this if I had succeeded in what I thought I wanted most in that moment of complete hopelessness, to no longer exist in this world.

Not only would I have missed out on all these events and people, but I would have missed out on ever hearing the most beautiful angelic little voices saying "Grandmama!" I know that no one looks into my children's or my grandchildren's eyes the way I do! No one! No one else can or ever will. This is what I was meant to do and there is nothing that matters more to me. I have to be here to do the things that only I can do.

Please, if you are considering suicide, consider your future instead. I never knew what I would be missing out on, but I do now, and I do not want you missing out on your enjoyment in life as well. You do not know what is in your future so please stop considering death as an option and consider life. If you have to fail at something, be a failure at destroying yourself and be successful at staying alive instead.

Send love out into your future. Picture what you might be missing if you go through with your suicide, and then magnify those moments times a thousand. I guarantee, you will miss out on over a thousand special moments that will make you thankful you failed at failing. Celebrate that kind of failure.

Please live!

CHAPTER 20

+ ◆ ◆ ◆ ◆ ◆ +

BREATHE

Just breathe. If you are having difficulty getting through your day, or even this moment, relax and breathe. One of my favorite breathing exercises comes from a book called, *Peace Is Every Step* by Thich Nhat Hanh. A simple breathing practice he suggests is that as you inhale you think the word 'calm' or choose a word that best represents the idea of calm for you. Then as you exhale, smile. That's it. Calm. Smile. Calm. Smile. I like this breathing practice because of its simplicity and the fact that it is easy to remember.

I have heard that the military teaches a counting breathing exercise for the purpose of teaching individuals how to calm themselves down in stressful situations. The breathing exercise goes like this: as you inhale count 1 − 2 − 3 − 4, hold your breath for four counts 1 − 2 − 3 − 4, then exhale to the count of four 1 − 2 − 3 − 4. This breathing exercise is also very easy to do; four counts in, four counts hold, four counts out.

Being aware of your breathing is important because it calms you down and brings your focus to what is going on in the present moment. This moment of calm clarity gives you an opportunity to decide what actions you want to take that would be in your best interest.

Try simplifying your life situations by just breathing. Do you breathe deeply? Do you breathe shallow? Do you breathe slowly? Are you hyperventilating? Notice your breathing right now, and then throughout your day really take the time to pay attention to it. Breathing is a part of your life you have control over. Relax, breathe, and obtain a sense of calm in your life.

From the time my children were little, I use to tell them that all they had to do was breathe, and I would be proud of them. I said this to let them know I did not hold specific expectations for them which they were required to fulfill to make me happy. I wanted them to be free to make their own choices in life knowing I would love and support whatever decisions they made. I used to say, "I love and support whatever decision you make" so often that one of my sisters told me I should have that etched on my gravestone. I want my children, and now my grandchildren to just breathe and whatever happens after they take this breath, is up to each one of them to control.

Please use these breathing techniques to gain a sense of calmness in your life. I will tell you what I told my children and grandchildren… all you have to do is breathe and I will be proud of you because I love and support whatever decision you make. All you have to do is breathe. Keeping breathing. After that, it is all up to you. Please breathe because with breath there is life.

Please live!

CHAPTER 21

◆ ◆ ◆◆◆ ◆ ◆

RESILIENCY

I greatly admire my husband's resiliency. My husband, Andrew Mueller, is a Lobster. Life has attempted to put him in a pot of boiling water many times and he keeps finding a way of crawling out of that pot one way or another because Andy is a survivor.

Most notably, Andy was the sole survivor of a helicopter crash while serving in Vietnam. Take a minute, please, and google: The Vietnam Veterans Memorial Wall, go to 'Find a Name' and type in: Ronald Frank Boeing. Andy was flying in a helicopter as the Crew Chief with his friend, the pilot, Ronald Boeing, on September 7, 1972 when they were shot down near Bien Hoa, Vietnam. Ronald Boeing was killed on impact, he was only twenty-two years old. Andy survived the crash and was rescued that day but suffered life-threatening third degree burns and major bodily injuries. He spent months fighting to recover at Valley Forge Hospital in Pennsylvania. Andy has lived every day for these past forty-eight years with physical crippling disabilities and pain from the injuries he sustained from the crash.

Andy wears a Vietnam bracelet every day with Ronald Boeing's name on it to honor his memory. Andy does not live with survivor's guilt because he realized early on that guilt was a wasted emotion that would not bring Ronald Boeing back to life nor give him honor. Instead, Andy lives his life and brings Ronald Boeing and all the other fallen Vietnam Veterans with him to honor them. Andy believes that what he experiences, they experience as well. This means Andy is going to live life to the fullest every day because they did not have the opportunity to do so.

Andy is right-handed. When Andy's right arm was seriously injured due to the impact of the helicopter crash, he learned to do things left-handed. He has a drive for excellence I have never witnessed in anyone else. In his later years now, Andy suffers with an irreparable right shoulder rotator cuff, his right arm is frozen in a ninety degree angle due to a shattered elbow, his scar tissue burns are still sensitive to sunlight and will easily burn requiring him to wear long pants, never shorts, even on the hottest summer days here in the desert. The amazing thing about Andy is that you would never know it by looking at him or trying to keep up with him because he goes forward without thought of his injuries and the pains those injuries create for him. It is only at night that the aches and pains catch up to him. Remember, Andy's goal is to live life to the fullest and he is not about to let an irreparable right shoulder rotator cuff, a frozen elbow, third degree burn scars, chronic back pain, both knee injuries, or prostate cancer due to exposure to Agent Orange to slow him down or dictate what he is capable of doing. Lobsters do not give up.

As his wife, the person who has been his closest confidant for the past fifteen years, I know Ronald Boeing and the other fallen Vietnam Veterans would be proud of the life they have lived 'together' these past forty-eight years. They would be proud of how he has loved, what he has accomplished, and most importantly, how he kept on living past all the destruction that was the Vietnam War. He lived for himself and he lived for each one of them in his own way. He is after all, the Lobster.

Please be the Lobster in your own life. Find a way past all the destruction to a place where you can live life to the fullest. At least for right now, make living your goal. Keep climbing out of the pot of boiling water to live another day. Live for yourself, and live for those you love. Just make sure each day that you live. Be a Lobster that resists death.

Please live!

CHAPTER 22

SURVIVE

Your task from this moment forward is to survive. That's all, just survive. No matter what happens in your life, no matter how insensitive or insane this world may seem, you must find a way to survive another day. Surviving consists of staying alive. The one factor that makes suicide so heart-wrenching is that it is one hundred percent preventable. So you must find that preventable way that keeps you from giving up.

You may feel as though you do not have control over your life and worse yet that what you do in life does not matter, but surviving is the one area where you have complete control of your actions. I understand you can't always change the way you feel but you can decide how you will act on those feelings. That is within your control.

When you begin to feel your life has no meaning or purpose and your thoughts start spiraling downward; STOP! Before you go from depressed feelings, to thoughts of hurting yourself, to self-destructive actions, step back and stop whatever you are doing at that moment. Suicide is not the answer. Please do not act on any self-destructive feelings and thoughts.

Sounds simple doesn't it, just stop. I know what I am asking you to do will be the most difficult action you have ever taken in your life, but you are stronger than you know. You have done so many difficult things in your life already, and made it through to this moment. Use whatever means you can to stay alive.

As crazy as it sounds to me now, I used to cut on my wrist. I did so to escape the emotional pain I was experiencing. What I wouldn't give to go back in time knowing what I know today, to be with my younger self, and tell her she matters. I would tell her she is just perfect the way she is. Most importantly, I would tell her to put the knife down. She never deserved to be hurt the way she was hurt; not by others and especially not by herself. She deserved to be loved.

I cannot go back in time but I can be with you in this moment and ask you to put down whatever means you are using to hurt yourself. You see, you matter. You are just perfect the way you are. You do not deserve to be hurt by others and especially not by yourself. You deserve to be loved.

Find a way to survive. In time you will come to appreciate the fact that you made it through the darkest parts of your depression. In time you too will find the gap so wide between the times you felt suicidal to the times when everything became manageable. You just have to survive long enough to get to a better and happier place in your life. Even though we have never met, I am begging you to trust me on this. Life will get better, you just have to survive to know that to be true.

Please live!

CHAPTER 23

‹ ◆ ◆ ◆ ◆ ◆ ◆ ◆ ›

RUBBER BAND

If you are experiencing emotional pain and you are physically hurting yourself as a way to cope, I may have a way to lessen your pain. For example, if you are secretively cutting or burning yourself just to get through your day, replace the knife, razorblade, cigarette, or lighter or whatever tool you are using to harm yourself with a rubber band. Instead of cutting or burning yourself to feel better, put a rubber band around your wrist and snap it when you feel as though you need to experience physical pain to lessen your emotional pain. Snapping a rubber band is painful, but it will not be as painful or dangerous as burning or cutting yourself. Also, it will not leave the scarring that burning or cutting does.

For anyone who has never been depressed, the prior paragraph about someone actually hurting themselves in such a manner seems unimaginable. Unfortunately this is the case for some individuals who suffer from major depression. When an individual is depressed, the emotional pain has to be released in some way, in fact there are times when the emotional pain becomes too much to bear, and burning or cutting becomes a way to distract themselves from their emotional pain. Individuals do this to themselves because the physical pain is easier for them to manage than their emotional pain.

The ideal scenario becomes creating a way to eliminate the emotional pain so you do not have the need for the physical pain. But until that happens, please consider lessening the physical pain however possible with the least amount of self-inflicted injury to yourself.

Please live!

CHAPTER 24

TSUNAMI

One aspect that surprised me when I was depressed to the point of being suicidal, was how strong the urge could be to want to kill myself. There were times when that urge felt like a tsunami, as though my entire world was coming toward me in one massive tidal wave and I was being swept away by suicidal thoughts. That urge to follow through on killing myself felt as though it was somehow completely out of my control, as though the urge to end my life took over and I was helpless to fight it.

When you feel this way, you need to take some deep breaths, count to ten slowly, and shelter in a safe place. When a tsunami strikes a town, people run for cover in a desperate search for a safe place to wait out the storm. The urge to hurt yourself can come on so strong that it will skew your judgment and you need to realize it truly is every bit as life-threatening as what those individuals experience in a real life tsunami. Therefore you need to be in a safe place until the urge passes, just as they need to be in a safe place until the tsunami passes. Please keep yourself safe.

Keeping yourself safe means doing whatever you need to do in order to stay alive. Here are some precautions for you to take.

Stop rehearsing your death scene so that it becomes familiar. When the urge to kill yourself strikes, if you have rehearsed your plan on how to commit suicide, it becomes too easy to act on that rehearsed plan.

Distract yourself with an item of significance to you. Back in the 1980's when I was pregnant with my first child, I was instructed in

Lamaze class to bring an object with me to the delivery room to use as a focal point during the contractions, I chose a baby rattle. The same goes for you in this situation, choose an item that represents something to live for; one example could be a picture of a loved one. Keep this picture with you at all times by placing it in your wallet. Then, when the urge to commit suicide strikes unexpectedly, you have something you can hold and see to focus on, and hopefully will get you through your urge to end your life.

If you are unable to stop rehearsing for your death, and you are also unable to distract yourself from that urge, then it is time to shelter in a place of safety which requires going to the emergency room. The urge to kill yourself can be so strong that the only way to combat that urge is with professional help. Thankfully we live in a society that has hospitals available and prepared for just such a crisis.

Make no doubt about this, the urge to kill yourself is a crisis and you need to take shelter and seek help. This urge for your self-destruction will subside one way or another, but you need to be alive to acknowledge your survival. Remember, stop rehearsing your death scene, distract yourself with an item of significance, and finally seek shelter in a safe place. This is the way to keep yourself alive during these challenging life-threatening times in your life.

Please live!

CHAPTER 25

— ◆◆◆◆◆ —

REMOVE DEADLY RISK FACTORS

Guns are an easy tool to use to commit suicide. This is not a commentary on the Bill of Rights 2nd Amendment of the United States Constitution, "…the right of the people to keep and bear arms," but rather a plea to remove guns from your residence if you are feeling suicidal with thoughts of using those guns to harm yourself. If you have a gun in your home, it makes it way too easy to go straight from a thought to a deadly action. I am asking you to store your guns with a family member or a friend for safe keeping while your depression is treated. By taking this action you are saving a life, your life.

Stockpiling prescription medications to have as a plan to end your life is also a major concern. You need to dispose of these medications to keep yourself safe. Use whatever method you want to dispose of them, but get them out of your home.

Another popular method for committing suicide is hanging. This method of committing suicide is popular because the items needed to complete the suicide are so readily available throughout one's home. Rope, electrical cord, wire hanger, or even a bed sheet are items people use as tools to hang themselves. I understand that it is impossible for me to ask you to remove all potential items from your home that you may consider using if you are truly contemplating hanging yourself. The only way to protect yourself from this type of death is to seek professional help as soon as possible so you no longer consider suicide by hanging, thus removing this deadly risk factor from your life.

Again, the focus and goal is to remove as many harmful risk factors as possible from your surroundings by making your home a safe place. The rest of the world may not feel like a safe place to live in, but your home should be your safe place. Create your own safe harbor in this world and make your home a place of refuge. Take away deadly temptations as best you can until you are stronger and know you won't be using these deadly risk factors to harm yourself. This is extremely important because your life matters.

Please live!

CHAPTER 26

TRYING TOO HARD TO BE PERFECT

There is a difference between striving for excellence and trying too hard to be perfect and here is one way to recognize the difference. When you strive for excellence, you work toward a goal with passion. You may fail many times along the way in your attempts to reach your goal but you do not give up and you consider every avenue you can think of to accomplish your goal. Trying too hard to be perfect all the time lacks perseverance; you may try but become easily discouraged and stop reaching for your goal altogether.

You need to relax and stop trying so hard to be perfect. By doing so you will find that the goal you are working towards becomes much easier for you to achieve. Take golfing for instance, the harder I tried to play golf, the worse I did. When I was consumed with being my husband's perfect golf partner, I approached the ball before every swing with a litany of instructions in rapid secession running through my mind; keep your head down, grip the club tighter, step in closer to the ball, don't bend your wrists, keep your arms straight, bring the club back like you are backing out the driveway, stop your swing at the top to gain control, don't forget to follow through; okay, now swing and hit the ball perfectly! No wonder I failed to golf well when I had all this running through my head prior to every swing. One day, I broke down in the middle of the golf course and started crying out of sheer frustration. I swore to myself this would be the last time I would ever play golf!

After all, I was trying so hard to be perfect without any success and I just wanted to quit so I did not have to endure this humiliation another second.

During the remainder of that round of golf, I totally gave up trying. I approached the ball with an I-don't-care-anymore attitude and to my surprise and amazement my golf game improved. I actually began enjoying being outdoors in that wonderful park-like setting and playing the remainder of that round of golf. Trying too hard to be perfect made it impossible to do this task and more importantly made me hate golfing. But with this new approach of no longer focusing on perfection, I golfed better and I truly enjoyed playing the game.

These same lessons can apply to your life. Stop trying so hard to be perfect. Live without the litany of what you 'should' be doing. Relax, smile, and have fun. Enjoy doing your best and don't worry about the results. After all, the important aspect is to find enjoyment, satisfaction, and achievement in what you do regardless of the outcome.

Give up trying too hard and let life play out with you as a part of it and not against it. Stay in the game. Don't give up. Don't quit.

Please live!

CHAPTER 27

THE MAYBE GAME

When I was depressed, I used to play a mind game I called the "Maybe Game." Perhaps you do this too. The Maybe Game goes like this: I would think that if my life were different, I would be different, and then I would be happy. During that time, being me was not working out very well because I was unable to find a way out of my depression. In order to cope, I would play the Maybe Game. Maybe if I were thin and beautiful my life would be better. Maybe if I were intelligent, richer, better educated, musically gifted, talented, or famous I would not be depressed.

I learned that if I obtained any of these qualities, they would not have guarantee a relief from my depression as I imagined. Perhaps you do not agree. You may even believe winning the lottery would solve all your problems. Think again. Happiness comes from a place of being content with yourself. You create happiness from within yourself not from things outside yourself. It comes down to how you value yourself and ultimately how you love yourself.

Don't believe me? Check out the Maybe Game below of people that, from the outside, looked like they had it all. They had those qualities I so desperately wished for but it was ultimately what was going on inside of them that made the difference between their life or sadly their suicide.

Maybe if I were rich I would be happy. A famous fashion designer, Kate Spade, had a net worth estimated to be between $150 to $200 million dollars when she hung herself in 2018. Money does not guarantee happiness.

Maybe if I were physically attractive, I would be happy. L'Wren Scott, another famous fashion designer was gorgeous, yet in 2014 she hung herself. Beauty does not guarantee happiness.

Maybe if I were famous and loved by millions of people then I would be happy. Robin Williams was a famous comedian and actor who was truly loved by millions of people all over the world, including me, yet he too hung himself in 2014. Fame does not guarantee happiness.

Maybe if I were musically gifted, I would be happy. Kurt Cobain of Nirvana was musically gifted yet he shot himself in 1994. Being musically gifted does not guarantee happiness.

Maybe if I were a star athlete, I would be happy. Andre Waters was an NFL football player from 1984 to 1995 who shot himself in 2006. Being a star athlete does not guarantee happiness.

Maybe if I were a famous chef and could travel the world with my own television show, I would be happy. Anthony Bourdain did all that yet still hung himself in 2018. Having your own television show and traveling the world does not guarantee happiness.

Maybe if I were a model, I would be happy. Gia Allemand was a model and television star on "The Bachelor," yet she hung herself in 2013 while she was on the phone with her mother. Being a model and television star does not guarantee happiness.

Maybe if I were a famous writer I would be happy. Ernest Hemingway was a Nobel Prize and Pulitzer Prize winner for his writing, yet he shot himself in 1961. Being a famous writer does not guarantee happiness.

Maybe being royalty would make me happy. In 30 BC, Cleopatra, the Queen of Egypt, killed herself by purposely allowing a poisonous snake to bite her while she was in absolute power. Even being royalty does not guarantee happiness.

These are real people who achieved fame, power, glory, and riches beyond the beyond. They had it all except what they needed most in life which was the ability to keep living. They were amazing individuals yet all their wealth, fame, power, and admiration from others was not enough to sustain them. My guess is that they lacked self-content and happiness in their lives. What is vital is how you feel about yourself, not how you value expectations outside yourself. How do you feel about your very core? What can you do to achieve beyond the beyond internal happiness so that you want to live? This is what you need to seek and find. I do not believe anyone wants suicide to be their legacy.

At the end of the day what really matters is the relationship you have with yourself. You go to sleep at the end of the day as yourself and you wake up every morning as yourself, which never chances. You have to learn to be happy and content with who you are.

Do what makes you happy. Seek internal happiness from whatever form that takes. Whatever makes your heart sing is always your pathway to your happiness. Do something fun you enjoy doing. Go play. Lighten up and enjoy your life.

Please live!

CHAPTER 28

DRUGS AND DEPRESSION

If you suffer from depression, the worst thing you can do to yourself is to use drugs and alcohol. It is a well-known fact that using drugs and alcohol only worsens a person's ability to think rationally when that individual suffers from depression. I fully understand this is going to be difficult for some individuals to do, but you need to do this for yourself to stay ahead of your depression. Being difficult does not mean it is impossible. You have conquered difficult situations in your past, this must be one of those conflicts you need to conquer to stay healthy.

You cannot easily battle depression while abusing drugs and alcohol. You must find a way to get the drugs and alcohol out of your life so you give yourself an opportunity to battle your depression successfully.

Do you know how it feels for people who battle obesity to see pictures in magazines of individuals who have lost one hundred pounds and live healthier lives? I do. When I was severely overweight, I used to marvel at those pictures of individuals who had found a way to succeed with an issue I struggled with for most of my life. This can be the same for you if you look for and find individuals who have successfully stopped using drugs and alcohol. One thought is that you can attend an Alcoholics Anonymous (AA) meeting to listen to people in your community who once could not imagine a day without using drugs and alcohol. At these meetings you can learn how they changed their behavior and are now living drug and alcohol free.

Drugs and alcohol will take you to self-destructive places you would never have chosen for yourself if you were in a sober state of mind. We are not our best selves when we drink too much or zone out on drugs. It is not even who we really are, it's a different, often a worse side of ourselves. Ask an adult who was raised by an alcoholic parent and I am sure they can give you evidence based stories of how their parents personality changed for the worse when they drank heavily which in turn made their lives intolerable.

Get to a place where you can be your best self. People stop using drugs and alcohol every day and if they can accomplish this then it is possible for you to do so as well. If you can't do it for yourself, then do it for the people in your life that matter to you because abusing drugs and alcohol causes so much pain to those who love you. You stand to lose so much by continuing to make the choice to abuse drugs and alcohol; you can lose your job, your spouse or partner, your relationship with your children, your health, and then ultimately lose your life.

You have so much to gain by letting go of the drugs and alcohol. By doing so you will gain back control of your life. Please choose your life over drugs and alcohol abuse and give yourself the opportunity to battle your depression drug and alcohol free.

Please live!

CHAPTER 29

⟡ ✦ ◆ ✦ ◆ ✦ ⟡

CONTROL WHAT YOU CAN CONTROL

I went into crisis mode the other day. I tossed a giant red ball to my two-year old granddaughter, and during her attempt to catch the ball, she fell face forward onto the tile floor and came up off the floor with a bloody lip. I picked her up immediately to comfort her as I reached for a popsicle for her to suck on to help ease her pain and swelling. I realize how vulnerable she is to life's bumps and bruises and I want to protect her by keeping her from having to experience anything painful. She is two-years old and therefore going to have to fall and learn to get up. She has to learn how to navigate her way in the world whether I want it that way or not. She has to learn to control what she can control, and so do I.

My granddaughter is so precious to me and I do not want to see anything bad ever happen to her. I feel the same about you. You are precious to me and I do not want to see anything bad happen to you either. We do not have control over life's bumps and bruises from falling down from time to time but we do have control over self-inflicted bumps and bruises.

Control what you can control. You can control your actions. If you could have in some way prevented someone like Robin Williams from killing himself, wouldn't you have? Or Anthony Bourdain? Or Kate Spade? Or Ernest Hemmingway? These individuals were precious just like you and my granddaughter are precious; they were amazing individuals and now they are dead. Living was something within their control. Depression is treatable which makes their actions to end their lives even more tragic and heartbreaking. They did not see their own value and worth, because if they had, they would not have destroyed themselves.

Control what you can control. Suicide is preventable and is the only real bump and bruise in life that is totally within your control. You need to take action to correct what you are struggling with so you do not focus on destroying yourself. It is the giving up before the cure that makes suicide so sad. Don't give up. Don't quit. Take control of this part of your life. Please, control what you can control.

Please live!

CHAPTER 30

◆ ✦ ◆ ✦ ◆ ✦ ◆

LIFE IS ABOUT MAKING GOOD DECISIONS

My husband, Andy, has a saying, "Life is about making good decisions." I think about his quote often when I am struggling with a decision I need to make, wondering whether it will be a good or a bad decision for my life. I know one thing for sure, no matter what other decisions I make in my lifetime, committing suicide is no longer an option to ever consider. Suicide is never a good decision for anyone, not for me and not for you.

Suicide is final. Once you make that decision and then act on it, you will never be able to make another decision. Never! One moment suicide may feel like the right decision but moments later a better decision will come along. If you have killed yourself, you will never know or be able to act on the better decision, the one that takes you to a place where you experience less pain and greater happiness. But you have to make it past the bad decision to get to a better place.

Viktor Frankl said it best in his book *Man's Search For Meaning.* He writes about his work with suicidal patients. He states, "...patients have repeatedly told me how happy they were that the suicide attempt had not been successful; weeks, months, years later, they told me, it turned out that there was a solution to their problem, an answer to their question, a meaning to their life. 'Even if things only take such a good turn in one of a thousand cases,' my explanation continues, 'who can guarantee that in your case it will not happen one day, sooner or later?

But in the first place, you have to live to see the day on which it may happen, so you have to survive in order to see that day dawn, and from now on the responsibility for survival does not leave you.' Years ago I held on to these words for dear life.

Viktor Frankl's reasoning is exactly why committing suicide is a terrible decision, and deciding to live is a very good decision. Give yourself that chance. Life is about making good decisions. Please make good decisions for yourself.

Please live!

CHAPTER 31

THE SMALL VOICE

Listen to the small voice in your head. When depression is at its strongest, there is often a very wise small voice in your consciousness attempting to save your life. It is that small voice you hear that is trying to steer you away from acting on the strong urges to destroy yourself. Listen closely to the small voice because it is the part of you that wants to live.

The small voice is the wisdom you need to hear to overcome the chaos in your life. When you are considering suicide, the small voice will help you find a different path, a way out of your depression. It will not be specific instructions stating, "Here is how to end your depression…" but the small voice does counsel you to reconsider the ways you are thinking about destroying yourself.

The small voice is the part of you that actually wants you to live. The small voice knows there is a solution to your problem. The small voice knows this is not your time to die by your own means. The small voice wants you to live depression free. The small voice is your voice of hope for your future so listen to the wisdom of the small voice and choose life.

There is almost a gentleness to this small voice. Where depression is violent and self-destructive, by comparison, the small voice is there to let you know that love exists in this world. Love exists in your consciousness as the small voice. The small voice knows love is always worth fighting for so please listen to your small voice and let it lead you to a safer place.

Please live!

CHAPTER 32

STOP THE REHEARSAL

When you find yourself beginning to rehearse your death scene, you really need to stop and focus on something else. Depression can bring about an unexpected role for you as a Director where you actually begin spending time directing scenes in your mind of how you would go about killing yourself. You fill the scene with props such as a gun, prescription pills, a rope, a tall building to leap from, or some other item of lethal means. You may also begin to plan the whereabouts that the scene will take place. Soon you have created a scenario you rehearse over and over again until you know every detail of how this scene, your suicide, will be acted out.

Stop rehearsing! Awake from the nightmare before it is too late. Remove the props from your surroundings because this is your life we are talking about. This is about your heart that wants to continue beating in your chest. Keep your heart beating by focusing on a vision for living, not dying.

How about a vision where you are the hero of the story? Why not? Picture yourself in whatever problem situation you find yourself in and create a scenario where you are the problem-solving hero. Do you feel the need to leap tall buildings in a single bound? Great, create that scenario. Do you need to see yourself receiving an award or promotion at work? Great, create that scenario. Do you need to find the love of your life, or repair a relationship you are currently involved with? Great, create that scenario. If you are willing to spend hours directing your death scene, why not use those same amount of hours directing a scene where you are the hero?

This is an activity my husband, Andy, used to do on his forty-five minute drive to work every morning. He would create scenarios in his mind of scenes where he was the hero. This helped him survive the thirty-eight years of working in the fast paced, cut-throat, auto industry.

Can you imagine the difference for yourself between directing your death scene versus directing an empowering scene where you are the hero? One is life enhancing, the other is self-destructive. As simple as this idea may sound, why not give this thought process a try and see if it works for you? Stop rehearsing your death scene and replace that plot with one in which you save the day. Saving the day is exactly what you will be accomplishing for yourself!

Please live!

CHAPTER 33

————— ✦✦✦✦✦ —————

TURN OFF THE TELEVISION

Turn off the television, or at the very least stop watching the news. World news shows give you a half hour of the worst events happening in the world and our nation today, followed by your local news shows that give you another half hour to an hour of the worst stories taking place in your neighborhood. It consists of bad news that highlights crimes, disasters, and despair. If the news did not involve drama, no one would watch it. Sadly, we live in a society that wants to witness the plane crashes, car crashes, murders, racism, terrorism, and other forms of violence; and this is just one night's newscast.

News is depressing and will only add additional layers of depression for someone who is already depressed. If you are suffering from depression, do not watch the news, instead turn the channel and watch something else. Do not participate in activities that make you more depressed, especially if there is nothing you can personally do to alleviate the pain you witness on television. Spend your time doing something else that will relieve your depression.

Have you ever heard of mirror neurons? These are neurons in the brain that cannot tell the difference between something that is happening in real life that you are doing, compared to watching someone else participating in an activity. The same places in the brain are activated. This is why people get so caught up in a movie or watching a favorite sports team. Your brain cannot grasp the fact that you are not physically involved in the events you are witnessing. For example, your brain does not know you are not actually scoring that touchdown you see on television. Now, can you imagine what your brain experiences every night watching hours of horrific scenes on the news?

Eckhart Tolle, the author of *A New Earth*, states that the average person who lives to be sixty years old, will have spent fifteen years of their life watching television. Fifteen years! Does that surprise you? It shocked me! I don't want to sit in front of a television for fifteen years of my life. Instead I want to go out and live my life and I want you to go out and live your life too. I do not want to be on my death bed regretting the things I did not accomplish because I spent too many hours watching television. How about you?

If you want to watch television, consider watching something that peaks your interest (not the news) or something that makes you laugh. Otherwise, please consider turning off the television and find an activity that reduces your stress and thoroughly delights you.

Please live!

CHAPTER 34

FAVORITE BOOKS

If you enjoy reading books consider twenty of my favorite books to help manage your stress, anxiety, and depression. I cannot imagine my life without these books because they have been instrumental in helping me navigate my way through life. I have read these books over and over again. I re-read the books when I am in need of reminders or inspiration on how to manage my life. Perhaps one will become your favorite too. They are listed in alphabetical order because I could never choose one over the other in importance.

- ❖ *A Course In Weight Loss* by Marianne Williamson
- ❖ *A New Earth* by Eckhart Tolle
- ❖ *As A Man Thinketh* by James Allen
- ❖ *Awaken The Giant Within* by Tony Robbins
- ❖ *Women Food And God* by Geneen Roth
- ❖ *Daring Greatly* by Brene Brown
- ❖ *Don't Sweat The Small Stuff* by Richard Carlson
- ❖ *Getting The Love You Want* by Harville Hendrix
- ❖ *Long Walk To Freedom* by Nelson Mandela
- ❖ *Man's Search For Meaning* by Viktor Frankl
- ❖ *Peace Is Every Step* by Thich Nhat Hanh
- ❖ *Revolution From Within* by Gloria Steinem
- ❖ *The Book of Joy* by The Dalai Lama, Bishop Desmond Tutu with Douglas Abrams
- ❖ *The Four Agreements* by Don Miguel Ruiz

- ❖ *The Greatest Salesman In The World* by Og Mandino
- ❖ *The Power of Now* by Eckhart Tolle
- ❖ *The Seat Of The Soul* by Gary Zukav
- ❖ *The Secret* by Rhonda Byrne
- ❖ *The Tao Of Pooh* by Benjamin Hoff
- ❖ *The Untethered Soul: The Journey Beyond Yourself* by Michael A. Singer

The Greatest Salesman In The World was the first of my favorite books that I read. It was given to me in high school by David Hallal, our guidance counselor. When he gave me this book, he suggested I read the chapter "I Am Nature's Greatest Miracle" every night for the next thirty days which I did. To this day I still have part of that chapter memorized because I loved the author's message and what it has always meant to me.

Peace Is Every Step is where I read about the breathing exercise I shared with my clients in counseling. The book is filled with calming principles. *Long Walk To Freedom* is one of my favorite books because of the extraordinary life of Nelson Mandela. His courage and enduring fight for his beliefs is as important to me as his planting a garden when that was all he was capable of doing while imprisoned. He made his life matter in both big and small ways.

If you are looking to sit with two wise Grandpa-like individuals and talk about life's most important messages, then I would recommend *The Book Of Joy.* The Dalai Lama and Archbishop Tutu sit down together for the purpose of having this book written. It is every bit as joyful and sweet a read as I have ever experienced and it is the kind of book you wish you could live inside.

The Power Of Now and *A New Earth,* both by Eckhart Tolle; *The Seat Of The Soul* by Gary Zukav; and *The Untethered Soul: The Journey Beyond Yourself* by Michael A. Singer are favorites of mine because these books are filled with an abundance of deep meaningful truths that impact my life for the better. I re-read these books as often as I can to help me focus on my life in a more positive way.

Man's Search For Meaning is Viktor Frankl's book about his experience as a Jew living in the death camps in Germany during WWII. As a psychiatrist, while struggling to survive in the death camp, he develops his theory of meaning called Logotherapy. Please know that if you are going to choose to read this book, it can be a difficult read because of the depth of cruelty inflicted on the prisoners in this death camp. Although it has a happy ending in the sense that he lived to tell about his experiences, it can be incomprehensible to read about the real life horror inflicted on fellow human beings. In the book, Viktor Frankl has an inspiring message for his suicidal patients that he treated after his release. I will go to my grave and beyond admiring this author.

Revolution From Within was my first introduction to the women's movement and one of its shining stars, Gloria Steinem. It taught me to look inward and love myself, especially as a female in a male dominant world. *Daring Greatly* by Brene Brown is a call to arms for all people to live up to their full potential.

As A Man Thinketh was published in 1903. I first heard about this book at a funeral for my Aunt Sis. During her eulogy, one of my cousins mentioned this book being one of her favorites. I went out and purchased this book because I had always admired my aunt and I was curious to see why she liked it so much. After reading it, I could see why it was one of her favorites. It taught me the importance of being mindful of my thoughts and the power that comes from that awareness.

The Tao Of Pooh is just a fun read. I grew up loving Winnie the Pooh, and to see him used in this wonderfully simple, philosophical way is enchanting. *The Secret* is also a fun and light read where you imagine anything in the universe as possible. I have my list of everything I want to attract into my life written down and placed in the drawer of the nightstand next to my bed that I look at often.

The Four Agreements is a book on the fundamentals of life. If there was ever a book that was a how-to-live-happier manual, this would be the book. Every baby born should be given this book to read and follow. If we followed the four agreements we would all be our best selves, so much less depressed, and happier with our lives overall.

If you ever struggle with weight issues as I do, any book by Geneen Roth is helpful, and especially *Women Food And God*. Another book regarding weight issues, *A Course In Weight Loss,* by Marianne Williamson is one I have read so many times I have lost count. Her idea that overeating is a form of self-hatred, and food we use to comfort ourselves actually harms us, is a great reminder that helps me keep my eighty pounds off that I lost. Any time I begin to gain the weight back, I reach for this book.

Getting The Love You Want has a communication exercise in it I used to counsel couples. It is the Imago Exercise, and it works because it teaches couples how to communicate with each other by listening and repeating what their partner has said, but with a very specific script. It also helps in relationships because it puts the focus back internally instead of looking at the fault in your partner.

Awaken The Giant Within is a good book for developing specific strategies for living successfully. I could never afford one of Tony Robbin's conferences, but I could afford his book. *Don't Sweat The Small Stuff* is a wise little book with all sorts of eye opening moments that lesson anxiety and helps me to see the world in a different light. Changing my perspective from anxiety to being less worried is a gift to myself every time I read it. My favorite thought from the book is, 100 years from now, all new people.

There are millions of books out there written with the intent of helping you and I live a better and happier life. If my book or any of my favorite books do not offer you what you are looking for, then keep searching for ones that do speak to your heart and soul. Read what inspires you to live another day.

Please live!

CHAPTER 35

VISION BOARD

I am a huge fan of creating a vision board. The future is unknown and the unknown will most definitely increase our fears and anxieties. When we do not know what is going to happen we fill in the future with negative events. We often imagine worst case scenarios for ourselves. Does this sound familiar?

A vision board holds pictures of what you want for your life. Fill your board with pictures of what you would like to have or experience in your life and do this as if money were not an issue. This is a time to dream big. What if you could have anything you wanted? What would you want? If your answer to that question is, "I don't know," then my follow up question to you is, "After, I don't know, what do you think you want?"

A vision board can be a fun activity to create at any age. You can make the board as creative as you would like it to be. Fill it with words that inspire something you would like to achieve in your future. "You are stronger than you know!" is one of the sayings on my board because it reminds me of my inner strength on days when I am feeling on the weaker side of whatever is going on in my life. Put statements on your vision board that make you smile. For fun put a pretend million dollar bill on your vision board if you want more money in your life, or a picture from a magazine of someone you find attractive and would like to date. If you have a desire to go back to school, put a degree on the board with your name on it or a picture of an airplane, cruise ship, or train if you want to travel.

A vision board puts positive thoughts and ideas into your future. One of my favorite books, *The Secret* is all about the law of attraction, which suggests you can create what you want in your life by putting those thoughts into the universe and drawing them to you. Then you focus on what you want the most. If you focus on nothing but depressed thoughts, you will get more depressed. Likewise if you focus on positive thoughts, you will seek and be more aware of additional positive experiences as they present themselves.

Years ago I created a vision board and it was fun to see all the things I had put on that board manifest in my life. For example, on my vision board I placed a picture of an older blonde haired woman with a ponytail jogging to represent me. Then I placed a picture of a young man who looked like my son jogging in front of her. Several years later my youngest son and I signed up to run the Red Rock Canyon 5K race here in Las Vegas. Would that experience have happened without the vision board? Perhaps, but it was fun putting the idea out there and then experiencing it later on in real life.

If you do not want to create a vision board because that idea does not work for you, consider writing out and framing your "One," "Five," and "Ten" Year Goals. Andy and I did this about one year into our relationship. We typed up our 1, 5, and 10 year goals as a couple of what we wanted to achieve. Years later, ninety percent of what we wrote down for ourselves we accomplished. Setting out goals ahead of you and framing them gives you something to see and strive for when you begin to lose focus in your life. It also reminds you that it is important to have future goals so you concentrate on having a future of your own making!

Do it your way. Create a vision board, write down goals and frame them, or come up with some other ideas that put forth positive thoughts for your future that you can visualize. This is a fun activity to see what you are capable of envisioning and what is created out of that vision.

Please live!

CHAPTER 36

❖❖❖❖❖

TAKE A HIKE

Get up and go outdoors for a walk. Being outside of a building with only the sky for a ceiling can quiet your thoughts. I run in a park next to our home as often as I possibly can and one thing I realized the other day is that I usually run about three miles before I am out of my head, and begin looking around at my surroundings. I begin by looking up and noticing the types of clouds in the sky. Then I notice the cacti are blooming. I notice the butterflies have hatched recently and there are an abundance of them all around me. I hear the birds singing and I see the hummingbirds feeding on the dessert floral nectar. I now see all this and more but it has taken me three miles and a little over thirty minutes to realize all that is taking place before my eyes. During those first thirty minutes I am deep in an imaginary conversation with myself sorting through relationship challenges, figuring out the why's and how's of recent events and what I am going to do about all of these thoughts. I am everywhere except in the here and now of this moment of being outdoors.

Then almost in an instant, my surroundings come into my awareness and it feels like I have stepped into an animated Disney movie. Hummingbirds follow me from tree to tree and line my pathway with their beautiful shiny little bodies that float right before my eyes. Clouds stretch out across the sky for miles and the mountains still maintain a bit of snow, a reminder winter exists here in the desert. There are branches of trees entering the edge of the trail that I high-five as I pass them by.

It is magical out there running on the trail in the park. For me it is as though I am running on sacred ground.

There are even quiet moments when I can swear I hear footsteps running with me. I imagine those steps belonging to a friend of mine that died from breast cancer a few years ago or I picture my brother, who died at the young age of forty-one from kidney cancer running alongside me.

I do not always run with the dead, most days I encounter an elderly gentleman who could very well be over ninety years old who runs rings around me. I run like a turtle and he runs like a hare. When he passes me, he always says, "Looking good!" as he gives me a thumbs up; to which I reply, "You inspire me!" and he laughs. There is the bicycle rider who always smiles, waves, and makes me feel like we have known each other for years. There is also a gorgeous young woman who runs like a trained athlete. One of my favorite individuals to encounter on the trail is a woman who has the greatest smile and kindest words for me every time we pass each other.

I am sharing all of this with you to encourage you to get outside and explore your neighborhood. What type of nature is out there for you to experience? Who might you see along your way? You will not know the wonder and the bliss that awaits you until you get outside and give yourself this opportunity to see what comes along your path. You do not have to run, just walking and taking in all the beauty that surrounds you is fulfilling all by itself. If walking a distance is not an option, find a park bench and observe your surroundings that way.

Ready for something silly? I play a game, when I am out running. I pretend that the universe is trying to tell me something by what the people say to me on the trail. Hearing "good for you" or "keep going" or "you can do it" really makes me smile, and I enjoy the run that much more.

So get outdoors and see your world from the perspective of a walk, run, or sitting on a park bench. Notice the clouds, birds, trees, flowers, bugs, dogs, cats, and people. Get out of your head and see what fun adventures await you.

Please live!

CHAPTER 37

$\leftarrow$ ✦✦✦✦✦ $\rightarrow$

BE YOUR OWN GOOD COMPANY

Loneliness can be tough to manage, especially if you are depressed. Being alone can give you a sense of abandonment, as if you are the only person in the entire world. You can choose different ways to handle your loneliness; you can feel sorry for yourself, but that is not empowering; or you could see if someone is available to get together with you; or finally, you could choose to be your own good company.

What does that look like? Being your own good company means you treat yourself like you would treat a dear friend or guest. Do you like flowers? Why not buy yourself some flowers the next time you are at the store? You can buy the flowers for your own enjoyment. Are you hungry? How about taking yourself out to dinner? Choose your favorite restaurant and have fun ordering a meal you know you will really appreciate and enjoy. Do you need a new outfit? Take yourself shopping to purchase a new piece of clothing that makes you feel special when you put it on.

Being your own good company means you entertain yourself with activities you enjoy that bring a sense of calmness and satisfaction to you. Perhaps you would enjoy playing a new video game, or gardening, or reading a book, or doing crafts? Consider going out to a show, concert, or movie. I absolutely love going for a run in the park because it helps me to clear my head and makes me feel energized. What energizes you?

The bottom line is to find what you love to do, and do it. Be kind to yourself. Pretend it is your birthday and make your day special. I had a co-worker that always took her birthday off from work so she could go exploring all by herself, whether it was a new area of our city or a different city altogether.

Still unsure what to do? Then try choosing an adventure that delights your spirit from the list of 100 Activities that are included in Chapter 46 of this book and see if that helps to dissipate your loneliness. Remember, this is a special time for a very special person, and that person is you! The specific activity you choose to do is not what is important. What is important is learning to be kind to yourself by becoming your own good company.

Please live!

CHAPTER 38

+ + + + + +

CRY

As a former Licensed Professional Counselor with a Master of Arts in Counseling Degree, with years of private practice, I am giving you permission to cry. I want to make sure you know I am qualified to make that judgement for you.

As a wife, mother, grandmother, daughter, sister, aunt, cousin, woman, runner, baker, pianist, seamstress, fisherman, golfer, bicycle rider, and fellow human being, I am giving you permission to cry.

It does not matter who told you in the past you could not cry. I am here to tell you they were wrong. People you loved could have said the wrong thing from time to time unintentionally, perhaps because they too were taught that crying was wrong or a show of weakness, and thought they were doing you a service by instructing you not to cry. I will say this again, you can cry.

Looking back at my childhood, my parents had an odd rule about crying. If I cried when I was young, I had to go sit on the steps leading upstairs and look at myself in the full length mirror on the landing. This was their way of deterring me from crying, however it never stopped me from crying, it only taught me to cry alone and not in their presence, which may have actually been their goal. I would have much preferred to be comforted and reassured about what was upsetting me because that would have been a better option for me. I promised myself I would not pass along this non-passionate tradition to my children. My children were allowed to cry and I was there to listen and comfort them. What were you taught about crying?

Crying is good for you physically and mentally. Letting go of your pent up emotions with tears is a healthy alternative to allow your body to release tension instead of holding them all in. I believe we are truth tellers. I believe your depression and anxiety will surface and do more harm if you continue to hold it in and do not find a way to release your true feelings. There are other methods people use to release their anxiety and depression such as overeating, starving, chain smoking, drinking too much, shopping beyond their means, gambling obsessively, or engaging in unhealthy sexual encounters to distract themselves from their feelings in the moment. The problem with these approaches is that the depressed and anxious feelings do not go away and an entire additional layer of new problems are added to their lives. These additional side effects together with their original issues, just cause more confusion, pain, and depression.

You may have a fear that if you begin to cry, you will not be able to stop. I know I have felt that way in the past. The truth is, no one I have ever known has ever started crying and never stopped. No one. Remember, I am a retired Licensed Professional Counselor, I have seen many people cry and every one of them were able to stop crying once their sad, frustrated, hurt or angry emotions subsided.

So the next time you feel pent up emotions begin to come to the surface, do not resist your feelings, let them out and just cry. Cry as often as you need to. You will feel much better having released your emotions.

Please live!

CHAPTER 39

❖❖❖❖❖

HOLD YOUR PILLOW

When I was depressed, my counselor at the time, Dr. Cruikshanks, suggest I let myself cry and release all the sad feelings I was keeping locked up inside of me. He also suggested I hold my pillow in a hugging sort of way, as if someone were hugging me back. I thought this was a strange suggestion until I tried it several times and was amazed by how well I was comforted by this technique.

The next few times I found myself in tears I would hold my pillow close to me and pretend it was my father, who passed away when I was sixteen. In my mind, he was letting me cry on his shoulder. This suggestion truly helped comfort me because this act of visualizing crying on my father's shoulder while embracing my pillow helped me grieve for him, and also allowed me to feel loved and cared for by him in return. These imaginary moments were all we had left, but they were very powerful all the same.

The next time you find yourself in tears, hold your pillow up against yourself like a hug. Picture a special person in your life hugging you back in that moment. Pour out your troubles and your tears to them as if they were in the room with you and see if that has a healing power for you as it did for me. It is just an idea. I hope you find comfort when you hold your pillow.

Please live!

CHAPTER 40

✦✦✦✦✦

TURN ON LIGHTS

There is a piece of artwork by Rembrandt titled, "Saint Jerome In A Dark Chamber," created in 1642 that depicts Saint Jerome in a dark room with just a bit of light streaming through the window. You can view this online at www.metmuseum.org. Please take a look for yourself at the obviously depressed state of Saint Jerome. He sits slouched, head tilted, with his hand up to his face, and his arm supporting his head while his other arm lies motionless on his lap. He looks depressed and worn-down. I do not know the story of Saint Jerome's unhappiness but according to www.franciscanmedia.org, "…Jerome is frequently remembered for his bad temper! It is true that he had a very bad temper…He was swift to anger, but also swift to feel remorse, even more severe on his own shortcomings than on those of others." If you have ever felt depressed, then perhaps you too can relate to the portrait of Saint Jerome in Rembrandt's artwork.

If you find yourself sitting in a dark room feeling depressed, please turn on some lights or open up the blinds or window treatments and allow sunlight to come into the room. Sitting in the dark serves no healthy purpose. It may feel right to you but it is not a healthy practice and will not alleviate your depressed mood. Flood the room with lights and see if that helps create a better frame of mind for you.

I had a friend who was depressed and diagnosed with Seasonal Affective Disorder (SAD), a type of depression that comes and goes with the seasons. Instead of sitting in her dark home during the cloudy winter months, she opted to purchase a sun lamp to keep in her living room. She discovered that using the heat and light from the sun lamp actually decreased her depressed symptoms.

We have nightlights throughout our home, several in every room, and it not only makes it safer to navigate our home during the nighttime hours but it gives me a sense of security overall. Being in total darkness is not pleasant for me nor for my husband. I know this to be true because it was his brilliant idea to place so many nightlights to aluminate the darkness in our home.

When you are depressed, light becomes important. Light your home with sunlight, lamps, nightlights, or even candles. Do not let yourself fade into the darkness. You control the light in the room. Control what you can control. Turn on the lights.

Please live!

CHAPTER 41

✦ ✦✦✦✦ ✦

JOIN A GROUP

You can be a part of so many different groups in your community. By joining a group, you get out of your everyday environment and meet new people. Often you will meet people you can relate to and doing so will help ease your depression.

If you are struggling with specific issues in your life, consider joining a like-minded group to work on your challenges together. Because managing my weight is always something I struggle to do, I joined a Weight Watchers group. The best part of going to the meetings is having the ability to interact with other people who struggle with the exact same issues I do. Group members share similar problem areas they are dealing with like wanting to snack at night after doing so well with food choices during the day. A comradery has grown between us as we offer support to each other while working to reach and maintain our weight loss goals.

A client I once counseled for depression loved to bicycle. We talked about the benefits of joining a bicycling club and he made the decision to join one, which was a huge stride for him to put himself out there with others. As it turned out, he met new people who also loved to be outdoors together enjoying the scenery as they peddled their way through their neighborhoods. He was so thankful to have found this group of like-minded people.

My husband Andy joined the Home Owners Association Board in our community when we moved to Las Vegas. He met many people in our community and has even made some very good friends. Andy enjoys the position and responsibilities as a board member and has developed a reputation in our community as the 'go to guy' with any and all concerns. In fact, one neighbor recently stopped by our home to ask Andy if he would be available to help his wife and son should a problem arise while he was away on a business trip. This group Andy joined has led to friendships that he values dearly and also offers him the ability to accomplish goals for the good of all in our community.

Joining a group can take many forms such as taking a cooking class, joining a book club at your local library, taking a defense class, swimming lessons at the YMCA, or joining a bowling league. The message here is to join a group that holds a mutual interest for you. The act of getting out of your home and being around other people in a setting that appeals to you will make a positive impact in your life. Finding like-minded people and new friends will be helpful in combatting your depression.

What appeals to you? Check with your local library, Chamber of Commerce, or travel site regarding your community to see what options are available close to home. Pick one and join in the fun.

Please live!

CHAPTER 42

———— ✦✦✦✦✦ ————

LIVE PERFORMANCE

Take in a live performance. Sit in a theatre and pay attention to the stillness right before the curtain rises on stage. The quiet anticipation of the performance right before the show begins is magical. Then as the curtain rises, energy fills the theatre as the performance begins. That energy will make you feel alive and connected to the entire audience. Having the opportunity to feel that energy and connection with the people around you makes the experience one that you will want to repeat again and again.

There is something special about a live performance. I do not know if it is because of the vulnerability of the performers putting themselves in the spot light or if it is because they are performing from a place where our collective hearts and souls meet as one.

A live performance has a magical quality for me whether I am sitting in a grade school gymnasium watching young performers sing their hearts out or if I am in a theatre in Las Vegas listening to Diana Ross, Cher, Alice Cooper, or Alanis Morissette perform. I love the energy during the show. The audience enthusiasm is contagious and I am always on my feet at the end to give the performers a standing ovation to show my appreciation for their efforts and my enjoyment of their performance.

Please do consider taking in a live performance. Choose a venue that interests you. My husband is a huge magic fan and one of his favorite shows is Penn & Teller. Find a performance that suits you. Sit back, relax, and let the show take you away from your troubles and worries even if it is only for a few hours.

If music or magic in not an interest for you, but sporting events are, then purchase a ticket and go see your favorite sports team play. Again, the crowds are energy packed and you can't help but feel the excitement of the game. Take in that excitement. Cheer on your team while enjoying the players' performance and accomplishments.

Buy a ticket for a live performance and see if that offers you a few hours of escape and excitement.

Applause! Applause! Applause!

Please live!

CHAPTER 43

$\bullet\ \bullet\ \blacklozenge\ \blacklozenge\ \blacklozenge\ \bullet\ \bullet$

RUBBER DUCKIE

"Rubber Duckie" is one of my all-time favorite Sesame Street songs. Ernie sings happily while taking a bath, with his rubber duckie and scrub brush in hand, while being surrounded by bubbles. He is having so much fun.

Taking a bath could be a very good idea to reduce your stress level. Giving yourself time to sit back in a tub of warm water, closing your eyes, and listening to soothing music will help you relax. The more you rest and relax, the better you will feel.

I believe in the healing aspect of water. Let your entire body sink into the warm water and discover the weightlessness that occurs. There is a refreshing quality to bath time.

You could even light candles or incense for some aromatherapy. A soft glow from a couple of candles, plus a pleasing scent will add additional layers of relaxation.

Pamper yourself. Totally chill out. Let your mind wander. This is not the time to contemplate problems and solutions, rather this is a zen time to clear your mind as best you can, relax, and de-stress.

Perform this bathing ritual as often as you can find the time to do so. For fun, you can always add bubbles and a rubber duckie of your own.

Please live!

CHAPTER 44

———— ◆◆◆◆◆ ————

WRITE A LETTER

Is there anyone in your past who was a gift in your life and loved you as their own? Was there a favorite neighbor, teacher, or coach that went out of their way to be kind to you? Perhaps this special individual might have been an uncle or aunt that gave you their love and support. If there was such a loving individual, consider sending them a handwritten letter to express specifically what they did to benefit your life and how that made you feel.

"Dear Mrs. Wetzel," is how my letter began. The Wetzel family lived across the street from us while I was growing up in Northeast Ohio. The Wetzel's had seven children, one was my age and one was the same age as my brother. We spent hours playing together. Summer time was a particularly great time to be over at the Wetzel's house where all the kids on our block would gather in their backyard to play on their monkey bars, kick the can, and tetherball. On rainy days we spent hours on their back porch playing Monopoly and other board games.

Mrs. Wetzel always welcomed us with a smile. She would have homemade popsicles for all of us kids on hot summer days along with a cold pitcher of Kool-Aid to quench our thirst and cool us all down. Mrs. Wetzel watched over us as a second mother and never minded playing that role in our lives.

Years later, as a mother of three, I realized what a gift Mrs. Wetzel had been to me and my siblings, especially because our mother had to work, which was rare for mothers in the 1960's. I decided to sit down and hand write a thank you letter to Mrs. Wetzel to let her know how much I appreciated all the hours we spent at her home under her loving care.

Mrs. Wetzel called me one morning after receiving my letter to let me know how much it had meant and how many good memories it had brought back to her. We had a wonderful conversation reminiscing about the old days in our neighborhood. We exchanged all the latest news and activities about our family members. I have only had the opportunity to see Mrs. Wetzel once since I mailed her my letter of gratitude. When I saw her on this occasion, she gave me a big hug and I snuggled into her embrace as I had done as a child. That moment of sharing between us is one I will never forget.

Writing a letter like this is so unusual. Who goes back after so many years to say thank you? This experience can help you focus on something good in your past and then bring that forward to share with someone that made you feel special in the first place.

Write a letter and actually mail it. The purpose is to send thanks back out into the world without expecting anything in return. Let the thank you be the gift you give back to someone special in your past.

Please live!

CHAPTER 45

DECLUTTER

Take a small area of your home and start going through your items in order to pass along anything you own that does not make you happy. We become so bogged down with all the 'stuff' we surround ourselves with that it becomes difficult to enjoy anything. Opening up space in your surroundings will give your home and your mind a refreshing new outlook.

This idea is not meant to overwhelm you but rather to help you declutter your life. Choose one small area to begin with, perhaps a desk drawer, closet, or cupboard to organize and then walk away having completed your goal for that endeavor. Organize your items by putting like items together. Find a place for everything, then put everything in its place so you know where to look for it the next time you want it. Throw away or donate items you have not used for years.

When you have the energy, choose another area in your home to go through and organize. You may not notice a huge difference at first, but over time your efforts to declutter your life will have a positive impact on your outlook, feelings about yourself, and your surroundings.

If you have items you do not use or haven't used in the past several years, consider donating them so they can become useful for someone else. What you no longer want can become a gift to another individual which makes this is a win-win moment.

According to psychologytoday.com, (Boyes, 2018), there are "6 Benefits of an Uncluttered Space" such as: it creates a sense of confidence, is energizing, reduces stress, allows mind wandering, can reduce relationship and family tension, and you often find lost treasures. What incredible benefits to obtain by taking time to organize and let go of items you no longer need or value.

Take time to declutter and reap the rewards.

Please live!

CHAPTER 46

100 ACTIVITIES

Individuals who suffer from depression have a more difficult time thinking of ideas for activities to pursue because their thoughts tend to be limited instead of expansive. I am offering you this list of activities to assist you in selecting and pursuing adventures to stimulate and energize you. See if one of these ideas appeal to you. Choose an old favorite or be daring and pick a new activity. Enjoy!

Please live!

- ✓ Amish Country
- ✓ Amusement Park
- ✓ Antiquing
- ✓ Arcade
- ✓ At-home Bath Spa
- ✓ Backgammon
- ✓ Bake a Pie
- ✓ Baseball Game
- ✓ Basketball
- ✓ Beach Time
- ✓ Bike Ride
- ✓ Billiards
- ✓ Boat Cruise Luncheon
- ✓ Bookstore
- ✓ Bowling
- ✓ Browse Local Businesses

- ✓ Bucket List
- ✓ Build a Playlist of Songs
- ✓ Build a Snowman
- ✓ Buy a Birthday Present for Someone
- ✓ Buy Flowers
- ✓ Call a Friend
- ✓ Campfire
- ✓ Canoeing
- ✓ Card Games
- ✓ Carnival or County Fair
- ✓ Casino
- ✓ Chess
- ✓ Chocolate Factory Tour
- ✓ Color with Crayons
- ✓ Comedy Club
- ✓ Comic Book
- ✓ Community Theatre
- ✓ Computer Game
- ✓ Cooking Class
- ✓ Corn Hole Toss
- ✓ Crossword Puzzle
- ✓ Do a Project for an Elderly Neighbor
- ✓ Donate to a Thrift Store
- ✓ Drive-In Theatre
- ✓ Driving Range
- ✓ Explore a New City
- ✓ Farmers Market
- ✓ Federal Park
- ✓ Fish Fry
- ✓ Fishing
- ✓ Fly Kites
- ✓ Free Concert
- ✓ Garden
- ✓ Go Out for Dessert
- ✓ Go Through Old Photos
- ✓ Go to a Local Park

- ✓ Go to Garage Sales
- ✓ Golfing
- ✓ Hiking
- ✓ Ice Cream
- ✓ Ice Skating
- ✓ Indoor Mini-Golf
- ✓ Invite Friends and Family for a Potluck
- ✓ Jogging
- ✓ Karaoke Night
- ✓ Legos
- ✓ Library
- ✓ Look Up Ancestors
- ✓ Make Your Favorite Recipe
- ✓ Mini-golf
- ✓ Movie theatre
- ✓ Museum
- ✓ New Restaurant
- ✓ Old Movie
- ✓ Online Quiz
- ✓ Orchard
- ✓ Paint
- ✓ Picnic
- ✓ Ping-Pong
- ✓ Plan a Trip
- ✓ Play Tourist in Your Own City
- ✓ Puzzles
- ✓ Read a Biography
- ✓ Read a Fictional Book
- ✓ Read a Magazine
- ✓ Rearrange Furniture in Your Home
- ✓ Rent a Video Game
- ✓ Roller Skate
- ✓ Sled Riding
- ✓ Soccer
- ✓ Stargazing
- ✓ Swim

- ✓ Take a Drive
- ✓ Take a Free Online Class
- ✓ Visit a Fire Station and Thank the Fireman for Their Service
- ✓ Volunteer
- ✓ Watch a Sunrise
- ✓ Watch a Sunset
- ✓ Window Shop
- ✓ Workout
- ✓ Write a Thank You Note
- ✓ Yoga
- ✓ Zoo

CHAPTER 47

DON'T WORRY

Remember the statistic I mentioned earlier in my book about people who live to be sixty years old having spent an average of fifteen years of their lives watching television? If I make it to the age of sixty years old, I may not be anywhere near the fifteen year average mark because I do not choose to use television as my source of entertainment. However, what occurred to me is that I have spent at least thirty percent of my life worrying about things I cannot control. Unfortunately I am a champion worrier, I worry for days and nights about life in general.

Here is the problem with that thought process, worrying never had the power to change what was happening in my life. Anxiety puts negative ideas into the future. I understand that the uncertainty of life can be very frightening and not knowing what is going to happen to you makes you feel out of control. People, including myself, do not like the feeling of not being able to control our situations. So, I have developed a bad habit of worrying way too much. I feel as though if I worry about something hard and long enough I can prevent future negative events from occurring, but the truth is, I cannot change what will be by worrying.

What I could not see until recently is that all my worrying never helped anyone, and only hurt me. So, I am learning to do something different. I am learning to focus on a positive outlook and then let life unfold as it will be, knowing I will handle the outcome to the best of my ability. I will deal with whatever comes along instead of projecting all sorts of negative scenarios out ahead of the event, at least this is what I am working with myself to do.

As an example, this week I was helping my husband, Andy, in the backyard with a project. It was a beautiful warm sunny day here in Las Vegas and I was wearing shorts and a t-shirt. After hours in the sun, I realized I had let myself get sunburned. Instead of thinking 'oh well it happens, next time I will be more careful' my champion worrier took over and started panicking about the appointment I had with my dermatologist for a routine check-up the following day. I was sure he was going to reprimand me for not using sunscreen and protective clothing. After an entire night of worrying, I went into the examining room with my guard up and a list of reasons to protect myself. My very soft-spoken and kind dermatologist came in, said hello smiling and began looking for any alarming spots that may have needed treatment. At the end of my examination, I apologized to him for having gotten so sunburned the day before. He looked puzzled and said he knew I didn't do it on purpose. Then he smiled at me, stated there were no issues to be concerned about and left the room. That's it. No scolding, no lecturing, and no 'You should have known better.' My champion worrier had gotten it all wrong once again. All those hours of negative thoughts for nothing and all they did was rob me of my day, my sanity, and a good night's sleep.

Take each moment as it comes knowing you will do your best. This is all you can ask of yourself. In the past, you have handled difficult situations. There is a saying, "The best predictor of future behavior is past behavior." Knowing you have successfully navigated the past life events, you can get through this moment now, and all the future moments to come. So please do not spend your time worrying about events you cannot control. Let your life be what it will be and address real issues as they occur. Don't worry. Enjoy your life in the present.

Please live!

CHAPTER 48

RELATIONSHIPS

If your depression stems from relationship issues, it can seem difficult to deal with because you cannot control another person's behavior, you only have control over your behavior. When the other person is not acting as you would expect them to act, that causes frustration, pain, hurt, and even anger. The problem lies in the fact that every person has their own unique world view. When your world view about something that matters to you, conflicts with another person's world view about something that matters to them, problems arise. How you handle the conflict makes all the difference.

There are some personal relationship issues that require you to walk away to alleviate your pain and suffering. Other relationship issues may be resolved by talking and listening to this person to see if an understanding of your different viewpoints can be reached. You do not have to abandon your view, you just have to acknowledge you have an understanding of why they hold their beliefs, and vice versa. There is a wise saying, "We can agree to disagree."

Perhaps you are in a relationship with a parent where your best course of action is to put distance between the two of you in order to protect yourself from abuse, criticism, or hurt. As badly as you may wish for a different type of relationship with your parents, some parents are not capable of being what you need them to be. Their personality may not lend itself to being the type of parent you need or want them to be. It is acceptable to do what is best for you to have a peaceful and healthy existence.

Whatever you do, do not use your life to punish someone with an, "I'll show them…they will be sorry," attitude. Suicide can seem like a way out and even a way to get back at someone for their cruel behavior. If someone has been cruel to you, your death will not teach them what you hope it will because anyone who hurts you does not have the capacity to understand or feel any sense of compassion for you. They most definitely will not see your suicide as their fault, instead they will do what they have always done and put all the blame on you.

You can always walk away from a bad relationship. If you leave a relationship, you have opened up a space to fill with someone who is right for you. I had to divorce my ex-husband to create a space in my life to have met and married my husband and soulmate, Andy. In my past marriage there were so many times I wanted to "leave" my first husband, but my way of leaving was to end my life. Thankfully, I survived and ended that marriage and then met Andy. The two of us are much more compatible and share many beliefs and interests. Most importantly we are kind to each other, respect each other, and really love each other on a deep and meaningful level.

So if you are dealing with a difficult relationship in your life which makes you feel like you want to escape by any means possible, even to the point of being suicidal, then walk away. Get out of any abusive relationship. Do not allow a relationship with one human being to rob you of the happiness you are entitled to experience. You deserve a big happy healthy life.

Please live!

CHAPTER 49

LOVE YOUR TOES

I once knew a person named Robin who I worked with at a college in the Office of Student Affairs. She was a person I admired because she was kindhearted, a leader, a hard worker, and most definitely fun to be around. Once, I walked into my office and found a huge sign on the side of my desk that read, "You're a Peach" with notes signed by all the Resident Assistants. I learned that Robin had organized this surprise and it gave me confidence that I was doing a good job as the Administrative Assistant for Residence Life. This kind gesture meant so much to me, even more than she would ever know.

I do not know why this sticks out in my memory, but I recall an afternoon at work when a group of us were talking, and Robin shared that she hated her toes. She said she hated the way her toes looked and thought they were very ugly. I had never thought about my toes as I spent hours of my life internally criticizing many other parts of my body.

What I was not aware of on that afternoon was that Robin suffered from depression. I believe her hating her toes was just the tip of the iceberg. A few years later, after I moved to a different State, I learned from a former co-worker at this college that Robin committed suicide. It was crushing for me to hear this news. She was so kind and so strong. It hurt my heart to think she took her own life and her energy and spirit are no longer with us.

I know now there was so much more to Robin's struggle than just hating her toes. The frustrating part is that somehow, some way, she did not trust that her life could be better from whatever she was suffering through. She never made it to a place where she could learn to love herself. The fact is, her toes were not ugly at all, and she was truly a beautiful person including her toes. The sad part was she could not see her own beauty.

So please find ways to learn to love your body. Learn to love your body's uniqueness. Each part of your body is so intricate and wondrous. Each of us is an incredible miracle of creation.

Next time you look at your toes, take a moment to appreciate their beauty. Learn to love your toes.

Please live!

CHAPTER 50

THE "NO" BUTTON

My husband, Andy, has a "NO" button. Push the button and you will hear a variation of "no." For instance; "No"; "Nooooo"; "no" (in a low voice); "N.O."; "NO!!"; "No no no no no no…"; "Nnnnnoooooo"; "No! No! No!" and "For the last time NO!" Andy had this "NO" button on his desk at work for some comic relief.

I would like to suggest you get a "NO" button, even if it is only an imaginary one in your head. Every time your thoughts stray toward suicidal ideas, I want you to hit the "NO" button. Once you start down the path of suicidal thinking, you may go from a fleeting thought like 'I wish I were dead because then I wouldn't have to deal with this' (whatever 'this' may be for you). Then, as time goes on your thoughts might begin to develop a specific plan to end your life. You may even go further and start planning the day, time, and tool or method to kill yourself.

At each of these stages along the way there are opportunities for you to hit the "NO" button and change the direction of your thoughts. Do not go along with your thoughts because your thoughts are just thoughts. They do not have the power to control you. You have the power to control you. At any point in time, you can take control of your life by changing your thoughts as easy as changing a channel on the television. All you do is push a button on the remote control and the channel changes to something completely different. Your thoughts can be changed simply by pushing the "NO" button in your mind and thinking about something else completely different. Choose a thought like you choose a channel, choose something you find interesting, entertaining, educational, or right down fun to think of.

When I choose a movie on television, I do not choose a scary thriller because I do not want to be terrified for my choice in entertainment and give myself nightmares. The same with my thoughts. I do not want to give myself scary thoughts. Dwelling on an image of killing myself is a very scary thought that often leads to nightmares; and is certainly not interesting, entertaining, or a funny mental picture for me to focus on. For me, that is when I use my "NO" button to change the direction of my thoughts.

When you first have thoughts of wanting to hurt yourself, you need to remember your internal "NO" button. You need to hit the button and tell yourself "NO" and not allow yourself to continue on with those thoughts. Then, you need to redirect your thinking from "I wish I were dead…" to thoughts that empower you to feel happy and content. So instead of being destructive to yourself, do something constructive and live through that moment to a brighter future.

The goal is always to live, that is how you know you are succeeding. Please live!

CHAPTER 51

◆◆◆◆◆

DO NOT ASSUME

During my counseling training, I learned about a case of a young college student who came very close to ending his life because of making a false assumption. This student was the first person in his family to be graduating from college and his family was so proud of him. His parents invited relatives and friends to their home for his graduation weekend so a huge celebration could take place in his honor. The invitations were mailed and airline tickets purchased.

A few days before his graduation party, this student found out he had failed one final exam that would keep him from graduating. He was deeply depressed and heartsick believing he had disappointed and completely failed his family. In his agony, the only option he could see in his depressed state was to kill himself. That way, he reasoned without good judgment, his relatives could still use the airline tickets to attend his funeral, and not have to incur further expenses because of his failure. Even in his distraught state he was trying to look out for his relatives' welfare.

This student made an inaccurate assumption that nearly cost him his life. He attempted suicide, but was discovered by his roommate and rushed to the nearby hospital where he was admitted and treated.

As you can probably guess, his family was shocked. How could he not trust their love for him? It was heartbreaking for them to come to terms with the fact that he thought it was better for them if he were dead than alive. He could not have been more mistaken.

Do not assume you know how someone will react if you commit

suicide. Do not make life or death judgements based on assumptions. As I sat in class listening to my professor talk about this student, I was so relieved to know this student's life was saved and his family rallied around him. Please save your life by not making a single assumption that has dire consequences that cannot be reversed. Do not assume.

Please live!

CHAPTER 52

✦◆◆◆✦

YOU MATTER

We matter to each other in ways we may never know. Just because we are not fully aware of how our actions influence each other does not lesson their impact. Your kindness and generosity of spirit is an important gift to the world. Do not deny your fellow human beings the opportunity to receive your gifts because you do not believe you matter. You do matter and your kindness to others matters to them.

During a period of my life when I was experiencing major depression with suicidal thoughts, I ended up voluntarily entering a psychiatric ward of a hospital to see about other forms of medication and treatment. My first day on the ward, I was so frightened by a very large male patient who became angry because the medical staff was not releasing him and he threw a fit right in front of me by screaming and tearing off his shirt. I was extremely terrified because I envisioned him attacking me next, which by the way never happened because the medical staff responded immediately to address his concerns.

At that moment, I wanted to be discharged from the hospital. The problem is that when you enter a psychiatric ward for suicidal ideation (suicidal thoughts), the doctors and staff will not release you until they are satisfied you are no longer a threat to yourself. I became so angry and frustrated with myself and my surroundings that I begged the doctor on staff to let me out, and he said "no." After speaking with the doctor, I walked out of the room and into the main hallway and began to sob.

One other depressed patient on the ward came up to me and handed me his box of Kleenex. He did the best he could in that moment to reassure me everything would be okay, then he walked away and let me cry undisturbed. As it turned out he was right, my medication was changed and my mood improved enough to be discharged from the hospital a couple days later.

To this day, I continue to look back with fondness upon this depressed patient who handed me his box of Kleenex. His kindness toward me in that moment was comforting and mattered to me in ways he will never know. He was a stranger stepping forward offering me kindness and I have never had the opportunity to thank him for caring about me in a moment when I was distraught.

The message here is that we come in and out of each other's lives in ways we do not even recognize. He may not ever remember me or the moment he handed me his box of Kleenex, but I will never forget him and his kindness, especially in his depressed state. We matter to each other.

Live so that you can make a difference in someone else's life, even if you never realize the full impact of your kind actions. Your existence could very well have an impact on someone you do not even know. Be there in that moment. Trust in your kindness and generosity of spirit.

Please live!

CHAPTER 53

SAVE A LIFE

I heard a deeply disturbing news report the other night stating that suicide rates are on the rise for children, five to eleven years old. As I began to research this news report I found that one in eight children between the ages of 6 and 12 have suicidal thoughts and according to the Center For Disease Control and Prevention, in the United States, 1,309 children between the ages of 5 and 12 took their own lives between 1999 through 2015. Sadly, I have known a number of adults and several teenagers who took their own lives but it never occurred to me that so many children at such a young age would be desperate enough about not wanting to live that they would act on those feelings by committing suicide. If it was within your power to save a child from killing themselves, wouldn't you do that? Wouldn't you even go so far as to risk your own life for theirs? Wouldn't you do everything you could to get these children help? I believe you would as much as I would.

Here is what I am proposing, save the five-year-old in you. Save a life. Save your life. If a five-year old deserves help, you are no less deserving at the age you are now. Age is not the factor, living life is.

There is no problem that matters more than your life. There will always be serious problems that arise, resulting in depression, grief, shame, embarrassment, underachievement, and failure; but none of these problems are insurmountable. What is insurmountable is suicide. The problem with suicide is its finality, there is no coming back from suicide. There is no saying, "I'm sorry, let me try something else instead." Suicide leaves no further options for you to consider. Suicide only brings an end to your life where you can no longer make any further decisions.

I believe that if you woke up tomorrow and your most pressing problems were resolved, you would not choose death. In your desperation to escape your problems and pain, you imagine an existence after death without any difficulty, or no existence at all; as if suicide would solve your problems.

What if you could find a way out of your problems in the here and now while you are still alive? It would be worth your effort to do so. One thing I have learned in my nearly sixty years of living is that life circumstances do change. How we face these changes is what really matters.

For the sake of the five-year old in you, choose life. Give change a chance by allowing yourself the time required for your circumstances to change and your life to improve. See if I'm not right and somehow, something changes and your life becomes worth living. The five-year old in you wants to live. Please give that five-year old another chance to make it through to celebrate your next birthday, and beyond. Choose your life. Save yourself. Be your own hero.

Please live!

CHAPTER 54

+ ✦ ✦ ✦ +

THE OTHER PERSON

He couldn't eat, he couldn't sleep, and he had recurring horrific nightmares. The image came replaying uninvited over and over again no matter how hard he attempted to focus his thoughts elsewhere. He could hear the gun shot and see the blood.

A family friend of mine was a police officer in a small rural community. Nate had become a police officer because he wanted to protect his family, friends, and neighbors. He believed a policeman was your friend. Nate was happily married with two small children, a daughter and a son. He was kind, quick to laugh, and genuinely a good-hearted person.

One Sunday morning, Nate was dispatched to the city park for a possible suicide in progress. He was the first officer to arrive in the park and quickly located the distraught man holding a gun to his head. Nate stepped outside the police car and with great care approached the man asking him to put the gun down but instead of complying, the man chose to pull the trigger and he killed himself just a few feet away from Nate. Within minutes, other police officers, firefighters, and EMTs arrived on the scene but there was nothing anyone could do to save this individual.

Nate was in shock. Being trained for such a moment is not the same as experiencing this type of trauma up close. Nate was severely depressed in the days and weeks to come, and most likely suffered from post-traumatic stress disorder. He would try to eat but couldn't keep food down; he tried to sleep but was plagued with reoccurring nightmares that kept him awake. His wife and family became extremely worried about him. I was worried about him too. After much soul searching, Nate made a life changing decision to leave the police force altogether to pursue a different career in order to cope and move forward with his life.

When depressed individuals think about committing suicide, they don't always consider who is going to be involved afterwards and what impact their suicide will have on the other person.

If you commit suicide, what will the individuals who witness or discover your body have to endure because of your decision? What will their life be like from that point forward? Their life will be impacted and not for the better. Nate is not the only one who suffered during this time, Nate's wife suffered, Nate's children suffered, the other officers, firefighters, and EMTs responding that morning suffered, and I suffered too.

One suicide can harm so many people even if that is not the intention of the individual committing suicide.

If you are suicidal, please stop and consider the life-long harm you will cause the other person. Do not multiply the sadness. Find another way out of your pain for everyone's sake.

Please live!

CHAPTER 55

PRETEND

What would it be like for you to not feel suicidal or depressed? Imagine for a moment you are not depressed. What would that look like for you? How would you feel? What kind of thoughts would you have as a non-depressed person? What would you be doing if you were not depressed?

If you are not sure, that's okay. Just begin to imagine what a happier day would look like for you. How would it differ from a depressed day? Write it down. Get a piece of paper and divide it in half, write 'Depressed' on one side and 'Happy' on the other side. Start listing your thoughts on either column.

For example, on the 'Depressed' side you might put: sleep in, not sleep at all, overeat, stop eating, think about ways of hurting yourself, going to bed early, call in sick to work, cancel an invitation to go out, watch television or play video games for hours, isolate yourself, cry, and drink and do drugs so you don't have to think any more.

Then on the 'Happy' side write down what that would look like for you. For instance eating healthy, exercising, going to work and making a difference, caring about good hygiene, spending time with your family and friends, participating in an activity such as a sporting event or concert, and getting a good restful sleep.

The idea here is to begin to take actions based on becoming an individual who lives without depression, a person who lives a happy, fulfilled life. When I was in counseling with Dr. Cruikshanks, he told me there was a time in his life when he was depressed. One day he decided to turn his life around by going back to school. He enrolled in college and decided to pretend to be an 'A' student. He did what he thought 'A' students did; he sat in the front row of the classroom, participated when the professor asked questions, studied the material presented, read the chapters assigned, took a lot of notes, and prepared for tests by studying ahead of time and not waiting until the last minute to cram for an exam. Not surprisingly, he did earn all 'A's. He earned enough 'A's to have the confidence to go on and receive a Ph.D. in Counseling & Family Therapy from Saint Louis University; something he had never expected to be able to accomplish. All this achievement because he decided to pretend to be an 'A' student.

What would happen if you pretended to be happy? What could you accomplish with happy thoughts rather than depressed thoughts? How then, would you treat yourself? What would you consider doing if you pretended to be more confident? These are ideas for you to consider and see what works for you. What reality do you want to create for yourself? Let's pretend and find out.

Please live!

CHAPTER 56

✦✦✦✦✦

100 WORDS

Sometimes when people are depressed, their vocabulary is limited to negative words because of their negative feelings. I thought I would make a list of my favorite 100 words and ask you to do the same. What makes your heart sing? What interests you? What makes a positive difference in your life?

Putting forth positive and uplifting words in your vocabulary will help change your mood. What comes to mind when you read through my list? If a word on my list triggers a bad memory for you, which was certainly not my intention, literally cross it out. Write out your list of 100 words that invokes joy and good feelings for you. Hang your list somewhere in your home that you can see and refer to often. Keep adding to your list. Focusing on a positive vocabulary will attract more positive experiences because you are focusing your attention on more empowering words. You attention is a powerful force.

Please live!

My List	Your List
1. Adventures	1. _____
2. Ageless	2. _____
3. Animals	3. _____
4. Artful	4. _____
5. Assertive	5. _____
6. Babies	6. _____

7. Beauty	7. _____
8. Becoming	8. _____
9. Believe	9. _____
10. Bliss	10. _____
11. Bold	11. _____
12. Brave	12. _____
13. Calm	13. _____
14. Celebrating	14. _____
15. Change	15. _____
16. Children	16. _____
17. Coexist	17. _____
18. Comedy	18. _____
19. Communication	19. _____
20. Compromise	20. _____
21. Confidence	21. _____
22. Connection	22. _____
23. Courage	23. _____
24. Creative	24. _____
25. Dancing	25. _____
26. Ecstasy	26. _____
27. Empathy	27. _____
28. Enlightening	28. _____
29. Enough	29. _____
30. Entertainment	30. _____
31. Enthusiasm	31. _____
32. Eternal	32. _____
33. Explore	33. _____
34. Family	34. _____
35. Forgiveness	35. _____
36. Freedom	36. _____
37. Friendship	37. _____
38. Fulfillment	38. _____
39. Funny	39. _____
40. Get-togethers	40. _____

41. Gifts   41. _____

42. Giving   42. _____

43. Glowing   43. _____

44. Goals   44. _____

45. Grandchildren   45. _____

46. Gratitude   46. _____

47. Growth   47. _____

48. Happy   48. _____

49. Harmony   49. _____

50. Healthy   50. _____

51. Hiking   51. _____

52. Hilarious   52. _____

53. Holidays   53. _____

54. Home   54. _____

55. Hope   55. _____

56. Hugs   56. _____

57. Humble   57. _____

58. Imagination   58. _____

59. Inclusive   59. _____

60. Inspiration   60. _____

61. Intimacy   61. _____

62. Kindness   62. _____

63. Kittens   63. _____

64. Laughing   64. _____

65. Learn   65. _____

66. Legacy   66. _____

67. Listening   67. _____

68. Live   68. _____

69. Love   69. _____

70. Mindful   70. _____

71. Moonlight   71. _____

72. Music   72. _____

73. Nature   73. _____

74. Organized   74. _____

75. Peace	75. _____
76. Pets	76. _____
77. Projects	77. _____
78. Puppies	78. _____
79. Radiant	79. _____
80. Rainbows	80. _____
81. Respect	81. _____
82. Safe	82. _____
83. Singing	83. _____
84. Snuggle	84. _____
85. Solutions	85. _____
86. Stars	86. _____
87. Stillness	87. _____
88. Strive	88. _____
89. Strong	89. _____
90. Successful	90. _____
91. Sunshine	91. _____
92. Sympathy	92. _____
93. Tenderness	93. _____
94. Thoughtful	94. _____
95. Traveling	95. _____
96. Trust	96. _____
97. Understanding	97. _____
98. Visiting	98. _____
99. Wisdom	99. _____
100. Worthy	100. _____

CHAPTER 57

CREATE

There was a recent movie about the life of Steve Jobs, in which there was a scene where he comes back to the company he used to work for and suggests the department of people he is managing begin to create things. It didn't matter how good the things were they created, he just wanted them to come up with ideas and create something new.

I think that same idea is important if you suffer from depression, you need to create something that interests you. That something does not have to be so great it cures cancer nor solves world peace. I think we often stop creating because we do not believe that what we make, matters.

I am a strong believer in creating new thoughts. I certainly applaud individuals hard at work looking for a cure for cancer or attempting to negotiate world peace but those are lofty goals requiring specific talents and a tremendous amount of energy. If that is your talent, please by all means pursue your goals. For the rest of us, including me, I create what I can with the talents and energies I have.

For instance, our granddaughter was born deaf. At eighteen months old she received cochlear implants. Our daughter-in-law researched and found headbands from Australia that proved to be so helpful in holding the devices in place while looking absolutely adorable tied in a bow in amongst our granddaughter's curls. So, having been taught how to sew by my mother, I used my sewing machine to make my granddaughter a drawer full of different color and designed headbands. Once she had what she needed, I then began donating headbands to other families who have children with the same needs.

I also love to crochet. Our next door neighbor growing up, Mrs. Mathias, taught my sister and me how to crochet blankets. So now, in my spare time I make and donate baby blankets to a program in our city of Las Vegas that provides items to low income families. I am by no means saving the world, but there are babies in our community wrapped in the most loving baby blankets I can create.

I do not think we have to accomplish lofty goals to make a difference in this world, rather all we have to do is find little ways to make a difference for someone other than just ourselves. Did you know the Ronald McDonald House need people to decorate lunch bags containing the free meals they provide to families with children hospitalized? Using your talents to decorate brown lunch bags for such a great cause gives you such an overwhelming sense of achievement and creativity. They don't have to be fancy, just a smiley face will send a message of love and hope. There are so many opportunities for you to create, and by doing so, make a difference for someone else.

What can you create? Creating involves doing. It takes energy and time on your part and in return for your effort, takes you away from your negative thoughts. Please consider some type of creating that can take you outside yourself and make a difference to another human being. You might just be surprised how good that makes you feel. Create, what a great word that is!

Please live!

CHAPTER 58

SHOULD

Be careful as you navigate life using the word "should." I "should" be smarter. I "should" be better looking. I "should" be good at sports. I "should" be happy. I "should" be better at this or better at that. I "should" be like my sibling. I "should" be successful. I "should" be doing something important with my life. I "should" be rich. I "should" be everything that I am not. I "should" be loved.

Who knew "should" could be such a dangerous word? I used to use it all the time oblivious to the destruction it caused in my life. "Should" sets up expectations that are given to you often from parents, older siblings, teachers, coaches or religious leaders you trusted and looked up to in childhood. You were expected to follow the rules and by doing so, please the adults in your life.

Being instructed by what you "should" do continues into adulthood from your boss in the workplace, neighbors, friends, and even television shows. Everyone has an opinion about how you "should" be living your life.

As an adult, you now have the freedom to decide what you "should" and "should not" do. The only problem is you may have the voices of these individuals from both childhood and adulthood directing your thoughts. For instance, I went to a Catholic grade school, and I can still hear the principal from my childhood, Sister Elizabeth Ann, telling us we shouldn't walk on other people's grass on our way to and from school. To this day, as I am nearing sixty-years old, I still have a problem walking on any grass with the fear that I will be in trouble. What about all those other "should" and "shouldn't" ideas that shape my life? More importantly, what "should" and "shouldn't" ideas shape and control your life that you have incorporated from other people?

How about all the television shows that tell you how you "should" be living your life in order to be accepted. For example, what appliances you "should" have, what type of vehicle you "should" own, how you "should" dress, or where you "should" be taking your next vacation. Start paying attention to how others influence what actions you take?

Start listening to yourself when you use the words "should" and "shouldn't." What follows after those words? Is it something you need to retain or let go? What expectations do you need to feel good about yourself? Expectations that drain your energy, leaving you tired and depleted need to be discarded. The words 'should' and 'shouldn't' are red flags for you to pay attention to. You only have to keep what works for you and let all the other expectations go.

Please live!

CHAPTER 59

◆◆◆◆◆

NATURE'S COUNSEL

Do you have a place where you can go to seek peace, solitude, and comfort? Have you ever been awed by nature? Does looking up at the stars at night ever give you a sense of wonder and a feeling of security just for the simple fact that they are there? Have you ever stood and looked out over the vast beauty of the Grand Canyon? Have you ever felt the calm ocean breeze as you gazed upon the ripples of the waves gently cascading onto a beach? Do you love the sound the waves make as they approach the shore? Nature is a gift that offers us so much to explore and enjoy without wanting anything in return except our love and respect. Where do you go to seek nature's counsel?

The Sheep Mountains here in Las Vegas, Nevada, are my sounding board. Whenever I am dealing with an issue that I am struggling with, I pour my heart out to the mountains. There is a park next to our community with a 1.7 mile north trail, a 1.7 mile south trail, and a third area with ponds and trees between the trails. The entire park is so beautiful, filled with flowering cacti, trees, bushes, hummingbirds, jack rabbits, roadrunners, partridges, peacocks, bunnies, ducks, geese, and even coyotes from time to time. The back drop to all of this wildlife are the Sheep Mountains.

I run slowly anywhere from 2.7 to 6.1 miles on the south trail, depending on how my body feels that day and what else I have going on. What is amazing to me, is when I realize I have run a mile or more without ever noticing my surroundings because I am so deep into my thoughts and the drama playing out in my head.

Finally, close to the second mile of my run, I begin to get out of my head and into my body and start seeing what is actually happening around me. I look to the mountains for guidance, after all they have an eternal quality to me. They have been here so much longer than I and will exist long after I am gone. I look to them to tell me what I need to be doing with my life and my relationships. The mountains are awesome because they just listen. The mountains do not interrupt, they do not give advice, they do not try to solve my problems for me, and they do not tell me I shouldn't feel the way I feel; they just listen majestically. I tell them everything I could never say to another human being.

I also go back and tell the mountains when the problems I have shared are resolved and again they listen with their wisdom of ages. They knew all along my problems would work themselves out with time. The mountains have heard it all before from people who came before me, who also took their problems seriously and shared it with them, and I am sure they will listen to future problems from people who come after me.

The point is, to find your solitary place where you can share your problems with nature. You need to find a part of nature, such as animals, water, mountains, trees, flowers, rocks, clouds, sun, stars, etc.; a solitary place where you can be alone for guidance from the stillness that nature offers every one of us. Listen to the stillness. Listen to the peaceful moments when you ask for nature's counsel. Listen to what follows when you get out of the drama in your head.

Go to that place as often as you possibly can and bask in the beauty and stillness it offers you. And remember, this is nature's gift to you, embrace the gift nature offers you while you inhabit this extraordinary planet Earth. Be still. Look around you. Listen.

Please live!

CHAPTER 60

◆◆◆◆◆

SHADOW

Live like your shadow. I love my shadow. My shadow is a reflection of me that is ageless. My shadow looks like a five-year old and like a fifty-eight year old all at the same time. That is the wonder and mystery of my shadow. It just is.

My shadow does not worry. It could care less whether I am having a good day or a bad day. It does not care what my bank account is, or how many likes my picture receives on Facebook. It does not care what my grade point average is, or whether I am achieving my New Year's resolutions. It just is.

My shadow goes everywhere with me but I do not have to remember to bring it along. As long as there is light in my life, my shadow exists. It can be big or small. It just is.

My shadow teaches me to just be in the moment. If I am jogging, then my shadow and I just jog. If I am writing then my shadow and I just write. If I am picking up one of my grandchildren to hold in my arms, then our shadows unite and become one glorious shadow. There is something mysteriously fun about having a shadow. It is us, but silently so. Your shadow is your reminder to always seek light in your life and to just be.

Please live!

CHAPTER 61

NO ONE LIVES FOREVER

Let there be no mistake about this, one-hundred percent of us will die because no one lives forever. Death is not something we can avoid no matter what we think or how we feel about it; we are given one birth, one life, and one death. So if you are feeling suicidal, take heart, you will die eventually. However during the time you are alive now, you need to understand and figure out a way to stay alive as long as you possibly can.

The challenge is finding a way to enjoy your life instead of ending your life by your own means. You are going to die but now is your time to focus on living. You need to find a purpose to live for. Your reason for living may already be in your life. For me, that purpose to live is for my family and dear friends. I never want my death by suicide to hurt my family and friends as it would surely do. Find your purpose to live.

Life changes so quickly. What is happening today may be completely different from what is happening tomorrow so if you do not have a purpose to live for today, it will show up in your life tomorrow. There are people who undergo life changes in the same day. You need to be here to see your purpose arrive in your life and find your own meaning. What matters to you? What gives you a reason to get out of bed? Have faith and live for that purpose.

You will die, but for now let that be. Put death aside and focus on living. Right now place your hand on your chest and feel your heart beating. Your heart is beating for a reason. Allow time to show you the reason why your heart is beating. Keep your heart beating. Keep your options open and please live to embrace your purpose.

Please live!

CHAPTER 62

◆ ◆ ◆ ◆ ◆

A CALL FOR HELP

On some level, he wanted help, even if he was not aware of that on a conscious level. I know this because he called me on the pretense that he wanted to talk about having read my first book. But that was not his real reason for calling me that night, he was desperately reaching out into the universe for one last chance to find a way to survive in this world.

His name was Steve and he was my sister's co-worker from Northeast Ohio. As Steve and I talked on the phone that night, he shared that he too had a long history suffering from depression, even to the point of being suicidal. He sounded depressed as he explained his current circumstances to me. As the conversation continued, I noticed that Steve began to slur his words and was becoming more and more despondent. I asked him directly if he was feeling depressed, and he stated, "Yes." With a sense of urgency, I asked him if he was having suicidal thoughts, and he hesitantly responded, "Yes." In fact, Steve stated that he had just swallowed a bottle of pills. Before I could respond further, Steve hung up on me. I dialed Steve's phone number several times but he did not answer his phone.

Everything began to happen in what seemed like slow-motion. Adrenaline shot through my body as I realized I was the only person who knew Steve was in the process of killing himself. What made the situation even more terrifying is I realized, given that I resided in Anchorville, Michigan, there was no way for me to reach Steve in Northeast, Ohio. Worse yet, I did not even know his address. I immediately called my sister and fortunately she was at home and had Steve's home address. Both of us called 911 in the hope of getting emergency personnel to Steve in time. Once I knew the police were aware of the situation, I again attempted to call Steve several more times but he did not answer his phone.

I sat up all night wondering what was happening to Steve. Would the police and ambulance arrive in time? Steve did not want to die that night despite swallowing the pills. He reached out to me hoping on some level to find freedom from the depth of his depression. This reaching out told me he really wanted to live. He risked his life on the chance that his call to me would somehow save him.

I learned the next day that the police and emergency personnel did find Steve in time to save his life. They transported him by ambulance to the emergency room where he was treated for his overdose, then admitted to a psychiatric ward of the hospital for further treatment. Steve called me a week later after being discharged from the hospital and thanked me for all of my help. I was so grateful to hear his voice once again and know that he was alive and receiving treatment for his depression The last I heard, Steve is alive and managing his depression successfully with no further suicide attempts.

If you are actively suicidal like Steve was, please get help immediately by calling 911 or a person you trust to get you help right away. Steve knew me from my sister and from my books. He also knew I was a Licensed Professional Counselor he could trust to get emergency personnel to his home. There was still hope in his heart that by reaching out for help, his life would somehow get better. Please call someone you trust to get emergency personnel to your home if you can't get to an emergency room by yourself. Allow the part of you that really does want to live to fight through your depression. Do not give into your despair. Trust. Call.

Please live!

CHAPTER 63

LOVE LETTERS

Think of each of these chapters as love letters to you, not romantic love letters, but love letters all the same. I know that if you and I had the opportunity to sit down face to face and really talk to each other, I would like you. I would come to understand you and know why you have made the choices you have made in your life. I would know what was behind the actions you have taken in the past. Most importantly, I would know your heart.

I know this to be true because it happened over and over again when I had my counseling practice, Safe Harbor Counseling Center in Anchorville, Michigan. Clients would come in for counseling as strangers. I would begin the counseling process by doing an assessment where I would ask what brought them to counseling and then additional questions would be asked based on their responses. Over time I would get to know these individuals in intimate ways. I would be trusted with secrets they had never shared with anyone else until that moment. I would learn about their relationships and what made them happy, what made them sad, and what made them angry. The counseling session was a moment in time where life stood still and all the focus, attention, and energy in the room revolved around them. I came to admire my clients for their courage and perseverance. I valued them because I could see their hearts in the midst of their struggle, and my heart went out to them.

Given that I am no longer in private practice, I can no longer offer you the opportunity to meet and talk about what makes you depressed.

For all I know now, you may be reading this book at some future date when my life on this earth has long since passed. All I have to offer without being able to talk with you, are these words in this book. I can offer you some thoughts to hopefully lead you to a place where you can become happy and depression free. I can offer you suggestions on actions you can take right now to put your life on the path to feeling good about yourself. I can offer you my hope that these words make a difference in your life in some meaningful way.

To me, that is love. That is the best I have to offer you and I hope with every cell in my body this is what you need to hear. You matter to me because we are both human beings who only want to be loved. Please accept my love for you. See these chapters as my love letters to you and know that I care about you and wish you a pathway out of the darkness and depression you are experiencing, to a life filled with love and self-worth.

How amazing would it be if you and I could transcend space and time and connect in a way that you could feel the love I am offering you, and in turn, accept my love into your heart? Let's connect through the words in this book and allow me the honor of helping you grow stronger to achieve a life filled with love. If I could hug you in this moment I would. Consider yourself loved and hugged.

Please live!

CHAPTER 64

◆ ◆ ◆ ◆ ◆

FROM DUCKLING TO SWAN

In your depressed state you may feel like an ugly duckling who is incapable of doing anything right. The truth is you are a beautiful swan! You are a beautiful swan whether you know it or not because we are all beautiful swans!

If you had met me prior to my forty-forth birthday, I could have given you one hundred reasons why I was truly an ugly duckling, the problem child of the family, who was incapable of ever measuring up to my siblings. I was flawed at the core of my being, a mistake, and a failure. I hated everything about myself except being a mother. I deeply loved and adored my children and that love for them is what kept me alive. Now, fifteen years later, I still love and adore my children in addition to my grandchildren.

Today the ugly duckling is no longer a part of me. I know how valuable I am as a human being. I know there is love in the very core of me and that I am not a failure or a mistake, in truth I am actually quite talented in several areas of my life. I have transformed from an ugly duckling into a beautiful swan and this has nothing to do with my looks. My transformation is all due to finding value in who I am as a person.

Interestingly, at my mother's funeral a few years ago, people I grew up with did not recognize me. A cousin commented out loud in total disbelief, "Is this Debbie?" as I approached her. People who came to the funeral expected to meet an overweight, self-conscious, insecure individual and instead when they encountered me they were surprised to discover a completely different person. I was at a healthy weight, confident, and happy. What was different was I was no longer depressed. A total transformation had taken place since they had last seen me. My transformation began when I divorced my ex-husband and received counseling for my depression. As I began to heal, I grew to love myself. In time I met and married Andy, a wonderfully kind man who made a tremendous difference in my life. From the beginning of our relationship, Andy saw the value at my core that I never believed was there. Now that I was happy and depressed free, additional transformations in my life continued to occur and I grew more at peace with who I truly am.

My transformation compares to the difference between night and day; the same difference between a life filled with dark depressing thoughts versus shining self-confidence, happiness, and love. Instead of wondering if I could make it through the day without committing suicide, I now find myself attempting to accomplish everything I want to do before my time here on this earth is over, naturally, and not by my own doing.

It is possible to go from a life of inner darkness to a life of inner light. It is possible to go from believing you are worthless and you do not deserve to breathe air, to a place where you want to breathe long enough to make a positive difference in this world, a place where purpose and meaning now fuel each day. It is possible to go from an ugly duckling to a beautiful swan on the inside.

Being a swan is so incredible. You wake up every day looking for ways to help other swans out of the darkness they feel themselves trapped in. The truth is we are all swans whether we know it or not. We are all valuable, we just have to find our way to a place where we can recognize our own inner beauty.

Please do not kill yourself because you feel like an ugly duckling. Rather, embrace the beautiful swan within you!

Please live!

CHAPTER 65

ATTENTION IS A
POWERFUL FORCE

Attention from someone we love or admire is the best experience in this universe anyone of us can enjoy. Attention yields pure bliss. On the other hand, a lack of attention feels like total devastation.

When I was growing up, it was considered appalling to try and get attention. I used to hear people say, "Debbie's just trying to get attention," as if that was the worst atrocity I could commit. In reality, I desperately wanted attention because I was not being noticed at all; perhaps a little attention from someone would have not left me feeling so alone and unworthy. Not being noticed and involved made me insecure and less confident in myself.

Being unworthy of love and attention is a devastating place to be. The problem is, if you do not receive attention at home, you may seek it elsewhere and probably in all the wrong places.

By the age of nineteen, I was so sure I was undeserving of love and attention that I was willing to do anything to be accepted. I began a relationship based on doing anything for love which resulted in deepening my depression. The consequences were devastating when at the age of twenty, I married a man who was a sexual sadist because I fell in love with his attention. I mistakenly believed that his sadistic attention was better than no attention at all. It took me twenty-two years to build up the courage and self-confidence needed to finally break free from him.

Once I made the decision to divorce this individual, the freedom I felt was astonishing. I was free and ready to learn better ways to give myself the attention and love I deserved. I went back to school while working full-time and I learned to be more comfortable with the time I spent alone with myself because I became my own good company.

A year later, something wonderful happened, I met and fell in love with Andrew Mueller. Andy showered me with genuine loving attention I had never known before. He was all about wanting to really get to know me, and as he did, he valued my way of being in the world like no one else ever had. He saw my heart and soul, and embraced both of them. This way of being seen and loved was so astonishing to me that I was compelled to write about it and thus *101 Lessons In Love: A Couples Guide For Choosing Passion* came to life in book form because I had to express everything that Andy's love and attention taught me.

I deeply love my children and feel truly loved by them. There is something wonderfully grounded in the love between a parent and child, it is an eternal love that goes beyond our mere mortal lives. My heart will always live within their hearts, as they once lived within me.

This love from Andy is something much different and magically so. This love that we share has its place among the stars. Even fifteen years into our relationship, our love continues to grow. What Andy's loving attention has taught me is that I am a 'treasure' as he would say; because we are all treasures! We are all valuable! We are all worthy! We are all enough! We are all deserving of love and attention!

It is okay to want attention. If there is no one giving you the attention you need then give yourself the attention you deserve by taking yourself out to dinner, buying yourself some flowers, signing up for a class, learning to speak another language, playing a musical instrument, or taking dance lessons. Take a walk or a run so you can be outdoors in the fresh air. Do something to show yourself you deserve to thrive and be loved. Attention is a powerful force. Turn your attention inward and fall in love with who you truly are, a treasure to be valued.

Please live!

CHAPTER 66

＋◆◆◆◆＋

MY FRIEND ERIN

My friend Erin is a remarkable woman. She has been my very close friend since early grade school, more than fifty years now. We have been friends through a great many life events, and we care and understand each other on a deep level. Even though we have not lived in the same town since high school, we have always kept in touch, getting together when we can. Erin signs her cards that she sends to me, "Love and Friendship Always," and she really means this.

With her permission of course, I want to share a valuable coping strategy Erin shared with me. Erin was diagnosed with breast cancer last year and needed surgery right away. Following treatment for her cancer, she then required back surgery to relieve sciatica nerve pain that had also developed at the same time as her cancer diagnosis. She experienced a great deal of frustration after her back surgery because it significantly limited what she was able to do. Just the simple act of standing, walking, sitting, and lying down were extremely painful for her. Erin has always taken such great care of all the people she loves, and now she struggled daily to do even the simplest things. She was unable to lift, push, pull, or bend over. She could no longer do what she does best in life which is to take care of herself and everyone around her.

Erin endured months of rehabilitation. In the midst of all this, my friend Erin did not give up, instead she decided to write a list of all the things she CAN DO instead of focusing on what she cannot do. Her list began with smiling. From breast cancer to back surgery, she can still smile. Erin's strategy to come from a place of frustration and despair to a place of personal power is astonishing and speaks to her inner strength. I am in awe of her ability to choose an activity that gave her power over her quite righteous frustration.

Erin's CAN DO list continued with such activities as being able to brush her teeth; take a shower; dust; read; go for a ride in the car as the passenger; cut out inspirational quotes and hang them up around her home to motivate herself when she became overwhelmed; be mindful to stay calm because her nerve pain was affected by stress; and talk to herself about not allowing too many overwhelming days to go by in a row without being mindful to stop and rest more so she could handle all that she was dealing with.

Erin has always been a remarkable individual. I am privileged to have her as my life-long friend. Her strength is certainly an important lesson for me, and can be for you as well. Erin would like to think she helped you in some way, it would make her smile.

Would it be helpful for you to write down a list of all the things you CAN DO in order to focus your thoughts on empowering yourself to a better life? What is the first word that comes to mind for your CAN DO list?

Please live!

CHAPTER 67

CHILDHOOD WONDER

I once witnessed a remarkable event. David, the father of three-year old Lucas, stepped out of his vehicle and into a small puddle of rainwater in the driveway. As he took a few steps forward, Lucas noticed with delightful surprise that his dad had made these astonishing wet footprints on the pavement! With great pride in his dad, Lucas went from person to person in the driveway to tell them what his dad had been able to do! His dad made footprints! He said it as if no one had ever made those type of footprints before! For Lucas, this was a huge deal and he wanted everyone to know about his amazing dad!

David's footprint story reminds me of how much wonder children see in the world that we tend to dismiss as we age. Wouldn't it be wonderful to wake up every morning and be awed by the wonder that is happening all around you? I keep thinking that the sun rises and sets every day with such beauty, but how many of us take the time to see it? I am about to turn fifty-nine years old, that makes 43,070 sunrises and sunsets in my lifetime. How many have I paid attention to? Sadly, not nearly enough.

There are so many aspects of nature to focus on. Have you ever noticed how silly some animals look? Who thought it would be a good idea to create a proboscis monkey? Have you ever seen its nose? It's kind of funny looking and reminds me of the saying, beauty may very well be in the eyes of the beholder.

There is so much beauty in a single rose, daffodil, or daisy. Dandelions, even though they are considered a weed, are beautiful.

Clouds, stars, mountains, valleys, oceans, rivers, in addition to human-made structures like bridges and buildings can all be breathtaking. Have you taken the time to look around and be awed by such beauty?

When I was very young and an adult would ask me what I wanted to be when I grew up, I would respond by telling them quite confidently that I wanted to be a bunny. I long for that time when I thought anything and everything was possible. What a great childhood state of mind that was to live in.

I am asking you to embrace your childhood excitement for life. Do not take life so seriously that you miss out on the simple joyful experiences that come your way. Get excited about your ability to make footprints in the driveway and smile.

Please live!

CHAPTER 68

MUSIC

Music. Maestro. Please. Music can evoke emotions and memories; and take you to a place that feels like you are no longer even in your own body. Instead you are lost among the notes, melody, harmony, and lyrics until you are floating among the clouds and stars.

Music is a part of us internally. Our hearts beat to a certain rhythm. Chords can be heard throughout nature in anything that produces a pitch, for instance, in the songs of birds or even in the wind.

Music allows our stories of love, pain, disappointment, victory, grief, and happiness to unfold. Music sets the background for the mood of our emotions.

This is why music is such a precious gift to us. Music can actually take us out of a moment of despair and lift our spirits. Have you ever heard a song and had to move to the music in some way; whether getting up to dance, tapping your foot, or nodding your head? Music moves us physically and emotionally if we allow it to.

If you are depressed, let music lift your spirits whenever possible. Choose uplifting music that speaks to your heart. Please do not do what I did as a teenager and listen to music that focuses on sadness and broken lives. There was a song I listened to over and over again, "Alone Again Naturally." The lyrics are about suicide ideation. That was the last song I needed to be listening to in my depressed state of mind. Choose your music wisely.

Today I have a revolving playlist of songs I listen to as I run at the park four or five days a week. Often my runs are more about listening to music than about running. I listen to Josh Groban when I want to take my run extra slow and meaningful. When I want something with a faster beat, I listen to Motown music. I listen to Broadway music for the energy it creates because I know the words to the songs and I sing along with them. Then there are the blissful moments when I listen to movie music arranged and played by Noud van Harskamp. Those blissful moments are like none other. I feel like Noud and his significant other Lenneke are right there with me and I am filled with love by being in their presence once more, even if only their imagined presence.

Noud and Lenneke are from the Netherlands and very good friends of my oldest sister. Noud is an exceptional musician. Last year my sister invited them to stay at our home in Las Vegas while they were visiting the United States. Noud spent the first night playing the piano for us and it was so wonderfully moving that I cried. Now, I am able to recreate that outstanding moment during my run outdoors at the park. Noud's music comes through on my playlist as I am running and I send him and Lenneke good thoughts and much love. I hope karma works and they receive the bliss they give to me.

Let yourself enjoy music in whatever form that takes for you. Go to an internet site or app and choose your favorite artists, and listen. Music can be a wonderful distraction from depression as long as you choose the right songs that move you in a positive direction. Listen. Enjoy. If the music speaks to you, feel free to dance and sing along.

Please live!

CHAPTER 69

✦✦✦✦✦

JOURNAL

Sometimes you need a place to vent, a place where you can pour your heart out. What might be helpful for you is to put all those negative thoughts in your head, down on paper by starting a journal. Make it your book of how you went from the darkness of depression to a new place where more light and happiness exists in your life. Purchase a journal with a cover that holds meaning or beauty for you.

Use the paper and pen to talk about what is bothering you. What is causing you to feel the way you do? Who in your life is driving you crazy? Who is hurting you? What is creating turmoil in your life? Write about your sadness and frustrations, your anger and your hurt, then turn the page. Do not re-read the negative entries you have written about over and over again because this will only defeat the purpose. Write what is bothering you that day then turn the page. Begin a new page when you feel you need to vent your feelings. Remember this is your journal to vent and verbalize your feelings without negative feedback from anyone.

Also use this journal to keep track of what is going right in your life. What happened that made you smile or laugh? What made you feel good? What did someone say or do that made a positive difference in your day? If you start looking for something every day that makes you feel good, that will become your focus and you will continue to experience more feeling good moments because you are looking for them to record in your journal. These are the pages you need to go back to and re-read over and over again.

The best thing about your journal is that it belongs to you, and you alone. You have complete control over how best to use your journal for yourself. Your journal is somewhere you can go to express how you feel, what you want, and what you are dealing with.

On New Year's Eve, 2002, I purchased a journal and began this process of verbalizing my ups and downs. At the time I was so depressed and thought it was foolish choosing a journal to write in when I didn't want to think about having any future at all. My first entry was writing that it was quite remarkable given my state of despair to even consider a year of journaling. That journal became a window into my journey to finally build the courage to end my abusive marriage of twenty-two years.

This journal was my way of chronicling my path from submissive wife to a free and independent woman. I had an awakening that year that was amazing to see play out on those pages of my journal. When I began writing my first book, *Sadistic Love: My Twenty-Two Year Marriage To A Sexual Sadist,* that journal was invaluable because it showed me, and the readers of my book, how I felt and what I was thinking that brought me to that awakening. I had included counseling sessions, conversations with family members, and time spent in a psychiatric ward. It was total craziness and enlightenment all within the pages of that journal I purchased on a whim.

Please purchase your journal today. You do not have to wait for the beginning of a new year. Choose a journal design you love, one that feels good to hold in your hands and creates happy thoughts. Write whatever you need to write, whenever the mood strikes you. Write your story as it unfolds. Tell your journal how you feel knowing this is for your eyes only. Vent when you need to vent. Release the negative thoughts out of your head and onto paper but don't forget to write about all the good and happy thoughts and events for those are the most important entries to re-read. In a year's time, see where your journey has taken you. Give yourself that future.

Please live!

CHAPTER 70

✦✦✦✦✦

MOVE

Depression can cause you to want to imitate a rock. You may want to sit and do absolutely nothing because any movement seems to be more than you have the energy for. You need to fight this urge and move. By moving, I mean walk, jog, bike, skate, swim, jump rope, lift weights, walk up and down stairs, dance, run, play a sport, or even purposely park your vehicle farther than you intended to, just so you have to take additional steps.

If you sit in your home and do not get out and move around, you are adding layers to your troubles because inactivity causes problems for your muscles, joints, skeletal system, and most importantly your heart. Sitting keeps you from burning calories, and depending on how much you eat, can cause weight issues. Moving is healthy both physically and mentally for you.

What do you want for yourself? The choice is yours to make. Do you want to be happy and healthy? Do you want to be able to move around freely because this is what your body was made to do? Do you want the body you had as a child when you could run for fun without ever giving it a second thought? What do you want for yourself?

Moving keeps you from getting all sorts of health problems down the road. No one wants to be plagued with heart problems, high blood pressure, high cholesterol, diabetes, or disabling physical disabilities. Focus on achieving a body that does not feel any different than it did when you were younger and more active. The good news is you decide your fate by how much you choose to move now so make healthy decisions.

Moving offers the possibility of additional social benefits. Moving forces you to engage with life. The more you move the better your outlook becomes because of the experiences you will have. By getting out of your home you open up the possibility to make new friends and experience new adventures. Again the good news is that the choice is always yours and always available to you. This is an area of your life you control. Take advantage of all your opportunities to move and engage with others, by doing so you will improve your outlook on life.

Life is meant to be enjoyed. Go out and enjoy life. Find activities that bring fun into your life and add it to your schedule. Make moving a priority because moving matters and will improve your frame of mind and physical abilities.

Please live!

CHAPTER 71

+ ✦✦✦✦ +

GO PLAY

I am a Master Angler. I even have a patch from the Michigan Department of Natural Resources to prove it. Who knew fishing would become my passion? I didn't know because I had never gone fishing the first forty-four years of my life. I never had the opportunity to discover how much fun fishing could be until I met my husband. Andy came from a long line of fishermen including his father, grandfather, and uncles. He has been fishing since he could first hold a pole in his hands as a small child. In fact, Andy had his very own boat with a small motor at the age of seven.

When we met, I had no idea if I had sea legs. I knew it would be important if our relationship were going to progress past the first few dates. What I learned over time is that being on the water is the most natural, life enhancing, experience I have ever had. "On the water," as I call it, is my favorite place in the universe.

Where is your favorite place? Are you fortunate to have been born into a family, like Andy, that has always participated in an activity that brought you joy? Did you play sports as a child? Did you play a musical instrument, or have always wanted to?

What activity have you experienced in the past that you liked so well, that while doing it, you lost track of time? This is not something you do to please someone else rather this is about finding an activity that interests you, and you have fun doing it. Find something you can be passionate about. No excuses, this is the time to find a way to go out and play because your life depends on it.

If nothing comes to mind, perhaps looking through magazines would give you a clue to what holds some sense of excitement for you. Which magazine sparks your interest or curiosity? Find something you enjoy and then do it your way.

Andy and I fished with music playing and we frequently danced together on the boat. We wore silly hats and blessed the water with our light-up spinning magic wands. We fished our way. Our favorite game on board the boat was "Get the net!" because that meant one of us had hooked a large fish and needed help to bring it aboard. For forty-four years I never knew about the game "Get the net!" It was only in adventuring out and learning about something new that I discovered such fun.

Find your favorite activity, one that makes your heart sing and give yourself permission to go out and play.

Please live!

CHAPTER 72

GENTLY DOWN THE STREAM

"Row, row, row your boat gently down the stream. Merrily, merrily, merrily, merrily, life is but a dream," are the words to the nursery rhyme written by Eliphalet Oram Lyte and published in 1881.

There is so much wisdom in this children's song, "Row Row Row Your Boat" that as adults we totally miss. First, the song tells us to row 'your boat,' not someone else's, but 'your' boat. How often do we get tangled up in someone else's problems and drama? How often do we just want peace in our lives, but find ourselves caught up in the chaos caused by someone else's bad decisions? This song is telling us to get back and row our own boat. Look out for yourself and where your boat is headed. There is power in being in control of your boat. Keep control of your boat as you attempt to help others navigate their consequences from their decisions.

"Gently down the stream." What does it mean to go gently through life? When you go gently, you are allowing time for life to unfold in a way that gives you time to navigate the terrain. You have a chance to be still and look around at a pace that creates peace in your life. There is strength and power in gentleness. The song goes further to suggest we go "down the stream." It does not make sense to fight against the current because that takes too much energy and eventually we feel exhausted and depleted trying to make life something other than what it is.

"Merrily merrily merrily merrily." Life is meant to be enjoyed. Explore the world to see what makes your heart sing. What makes you merry? Roller coasters? Music? Hiking? Stargazing? Sports? Puppies? Sailing? Legos? Computer games? Movies? Holidays? Get-togethers? Biking? Children's laughter? Picking flowers? Donating? Cutting the grass? Painting? Creating? Golfing? Reading? Volunteering? Running? Festivals? Parades? Again, this is completely about what interests you. What makes you smile? Notice also that the word "merrily" is mentioned four times in the song compared to the word "row" that is only mentioned three times. So work less and play more!

"Life is but a dream." We often take life too seriously and miss the dream. Dream big. Dreaming is fun. Dream fun for yourself in whatever form that takes. What do you want for yourself? All you have to do is close your eyes and picture how you want your life to be. It's always interesting to write down your ultimate dreams and see what transpires. Remember to row your boat gently and merrily; and to dream.

Please live!

CHAPTER 73

UNDERWHELMED

According to www.thesaurus.com, underwhelmed means to "fail to interest or astonish." When you are overwhelmed by life, it is time to step back and disengage from the drama that is causing you to be stressed. Do not allow yourself to be interested or astonished by the drama of life events that leave you feeling unbalanced. Drama will throw you off course, and the more you interact with that negative drama the deeper your depression will grow.

So how do you disengage from drama that is causing you mental distress? First, be aware of your reaction to what is happening by paying attention to what words you are using to react to the circumstances. If you learn about something disappointing, use language that lessons the impact and creates less stress for yourself and everyone around you. Instead of swearing when something goes wrong, say something like, "oh darn," "fudge," "oh boo," or "shucks." These words do not have the negative energy associated with them like "oh shit" or "f-you" or even "god damn son of a bitch." When I used to hear that last phrase screamed, it made me jump and come running to fix whatever had gone wrong. That was the entire purpose of that message, to get people's attention and scare them into action. Now, I have learned I should have been underwhelmed by that last phrase and let it fail to interest or astonish me. I know that now. The person who used to say that in my presence is no longer in my life.

Always attempt to stay calm and be underwhelmed by life when you find yourself overwhelmed.

Please live!

CHAPTER 74

❖◆◆◆◆❖

LOWER YOUR EXPECTATIONS

Be careful about what expectations you set for yourself and what others set for you. Expectations you hold onto can make you feel like you are not where you need to be in life. Your thoughts that by now you should have accomplished this goal or that task just creates more stress in your life. Once I heard about a famous Violinist who was greeting audience members after his performance. One such audience member said, "I would give my life to play the violin like that." To which the Violinist replied, "I did." The Violinist sacrificed his life in order to focus all of his attention on his music. Would that audience member still have wanted to sacrifice everything in their life for this type of singular focus? I do not know for sure, but I am guessing not.

Lower your expectations in the sense of giving yourself a break. I believe in setting goals, striving to better myself and my abilities but not to the point where perfection ruins my ability to want to live. I do not want perfection to make me suicidal because I cannot live up to my expectations.

I once knew a dedicated high school Band Director who was married, and he and his wife had a beautiful baby girl they adored. There was a tremendous amount of pressure put on him by the school administration and parents to have the marching band win all their competitions. To this Band Director, winning and losing competitions became how he valued himself because of the expectations placed on him. Not being able to fulfill these unrealistic expectations, he opted to take his own life. Fortunately, his wife found him in time and he did not die that day.

The day he had attempted suicide, he was supposed to be attending a meeting with the board of parents involved with the marching band. The parents complained about him missing this meeting and in their minds not taking the marching band success seriously enough. They never knew he was in the emergency room of a hospital while they were making those accusations. The expectations he internalized from the parents and school nearly cost him his life. Did it really matter whether or not this high school won every marching band competition? How much more vital it was, that night, that the Band Director almost lost his life, his wife nearly lost her husband, and their beautiful baby girl came close to growing up without her father?

Lower your expectations. Put them in perspective. Expectations are not worth your life. Have goals and work toward them, but go slowly. You will find in time you do get to where you want to be. The best part is you will be alive when you achieve your goals.

The Rolling Stones stated this idea so eloquently when they sang: "You can't always get what you want. But if you try sometime, you find you get what you need."

Please live!

CHAPTER 75

DIFFICULT PEOPLE

People believe what the boss says about them matters. In the workplace, what management says about your work ethic effects how you feel about yourself. Ultimately you have control over how you feel about yourself, and that, you must always protect for your own well-being. So how do you do that? This is what I learned about having to deal with difficult people in authority. I worked for a non-profit organization as a Victim Advocate. We had an Open House where individuals and families we served were invited to attend. Our own families were invited as well. This Open House was a major event. My boss, the Director of the program for the State of Michigan gave an opening speech. She began by introducing the staff to the audience. One of those individuals in the audience was my husband, Andy.

My boss introduced several Victim Advocates by singing their praises about the work they did with victims. I could not have agreed more with her statements because my co-workers were exceptionally caring individuals who took their jobs to heart. I was getting nervous knowing she would be talking about me next. When it was my turn to be introduced she stated, "Deborah vacuumed the office," then continued on to praise the outstanding work performed by the remaining Victim Advocates in the room. I was shocked, embarrassed, and hurt.

After the Open House, I was walking out with Andy and I could not wait to hear what he thought about how she had treated me. She had deliberately unacknowledged any meaningful work I had accomplished. I was shocked when Andy said, "It doesn't matter."

Surprised by his response, I asked Andy how it could possibly not matter. I didn't understand. He explained that what my boss had to say about any subject, even my work ethic and dedication, did not matter to him because he did not respect her to begin with. He knew what I had been going through at work under her mismanagement, and he did not give her words any value. Therefore her words could not hurt him because they didn't matter. He took her power away by using this thought process.

Huge lesson for me that day. I began to give her words and actions less and less power over my thoughts in the workplace. I was respectful to her but I no longer let her words and actions bother me. A day came when the national overseers of our organization became aware of her mismanagement issues in our organization and they went through a process of interviewing every employee in the office. After several days of interviewing the staff they made the decision to fire the Director because of her mismanagement and lack of compassion toward her staff. The Director had her position and power over us completely taken away.

How someone treats you is not about you, it is about them. Andy's lesson to me that "It doesn't matter," can also be a lesson for you. If there is someone in your life that is disturbing your internal peace, do not allow what they say to matter and hurt you. You can be respectful without letting them control how you feel about what they are saying. You cannot control what comes out of their mouth, but you can control how you feel about it. "It doesn't matter," are great words to live by with difficult people.

No matter what happens, or what someone says to you or about you, it only matters if you let it matter. You know the truth of your situation. Eventually, it has been my experience that karma gives back to the person what they gave out. You don't have to seek revenge, let it go because karma will eventually come around and rectify the wrong doing. Remember this, it doesn't matter what people say about you, what is important is what you know to be true about yourself.

Please live!

CHAPTER 76

•✦✦✦✦•

THE PAST

The past difficulties, cruelties, and misunderstandings that we have endured have a significant impact on our lives today if we allow it to do so. The good news is that we have complete control over whether we allow the past to plague our lives in the present moment and continue to disturb our inner peace.

Part of my recovery from depression came from learning to leave the past alone in a way that it cannot, and does not, hurt me anymore, most importantly because the past no longer matters to me. I no longer spend my cherished time in the present dwelling on the past. I learned that the past can stay in the past if you allow it to. I have had to make peace with my past in order to experience an extraordinary life today.

I realized I had left the past behind during a conversation with one of my sisters when she apologized to me for some things that had happened between us years ago when we were children. These conflicts between us bothered me so much when I was younger that I let it ruin my life at times. It occurred to me during our conversation that whatever transpired between us years ago no longer held any relevance to me in my current life. I had let the past go and no longer allowed it to hurt me.

A lot of my emotional pain centered on our family dynamics. I was the fourth girl in my family. Being the fourth girl was like having a fourth piece of cake for my parents. After consuming three pieces, you wish you hadn't taken a fourth piece. That fourth piece does not have the same appeal the first, second, or third pieces had. Two years later, their dream came true when my brother, their first and only son, was born.

Our entire family dynamics changed with his birth. He was the 'sun' that we revolved around. My parents adored him above all their other children and that can be difficult when you are the runt of the litter instead of the trophy child. I was so depressed that I spent my teenage years participating in secretive ways of hurting myself. I began overeating, cutting on my wrist, wishing I would fall out of a moving vehicle, and even running away attempting to spare my family the pain and embarrassment of me having to be a part of their lives.

The most important thing I have learned over time is that my parents did love me to the best of their abilities. They really did the best they knew how to do. Parents do make unintentional mistakes. My parents' thoughts and feelings about me are no longer my thoughts and feelings about myself. I am not the runt of the litter, I am a treasure because we are all treasures.

The greatest aspect about the present moment is that you have an opportunity to focus on whatever you want, not what anyone else wants for you. The freedom that comes from knowing and accepting that thought is life changing.

So when my sister apologized, I realized in that moment I had moved way beyond all the emotional pain from my childhood and I was able to share that realization with her. Together, we moved forward with a better understanding and love for each other.

I am not asking you to pretend the past didn't happen. I am asking if you can recognize that the past does not have to ruin your present circumstances? Each new day brings new possibilities. Can you let go of what others thought and felt about you? Can you appreciate the freedom that comes from discarding the emotional pain you have carried through the years? Put your energy and focus in the present, which is where you have the control to make a difference in your life.

Please live!

CHAPTER 77

✦✦✦✦✦✦✦

ANGER

How do you express your anger? Who taught you about anger? Have you ever thought about it before? Give it some thought as you read through this chapter to discover your feelings about anger and how it has impacted your life.

For so many years I did not know what to do with my anger. I was taught to be nice. Expressing anger was not tolerated in my family. We were not allowed to upset my father because of his heart issues. We were taught that any expression of anger could cause his death. When expressing anger becomes a matter of life or death, one learns not to show any emotion remotely linked to anger. My anger had nowhere else to go so I turned my anger inward on myself while maintaining a smile on the outside. This was not something I thought about at the time or even realized I was doing.

How sad that my teenage years were spent cutting on my wrist in order to have some control over the emotional pain I was feeling. Cutting is a way of bleeding out the pain in a literal sense. Ultimately we are truth tellers and cutting was my way of telling my truth about the anger and frustration I felt. Even though I hid the scars from everyone, to me, the scars represented an outward sign of how I was truly feeling on the inside. Cutting was my way of making myself feel better because it was pain I could control.

How do you go from self-inflicting pain to a place where you no longer need to cut yourself in order to control the emotional pain? As difficult as this may sound, it is learning to express your anger outward appropriately. Doing so at first may feel like a life or death decision. When you express your anger outward there will most certainly be someone who does not like it. I can guarantee if you begin to express anger outward there will be people trying to get you to keep your anger to yourself. This is where you have to begin to be courageous enough to stick up for yourself, your sanity, and place your anger where it belongs.

I had a counselor named Dr. Cruikshanks that I was seeing when I was struggling to survive during my first marriage. He used to tell me that I needed to put my anger with the perpetrator and not with myself as I had continued to do. He told me I had the right to be angry, which was an entirely new concept for me; and I had the right to express that anger toward my husband when he hurt me.

I began to find my own voice, and then to use it when a boundary was crossed in my marriage. Imagine my husband's surprise! First my husband would get angry and yell at me in an attempt to put me back in a submissive role that I had accepted in the past. That tactic no longer worked because I was not afraid of anger, not his, and especially not mine. I learned it was okay to be angry and express my anger outwardly in appropriate ways. The best part was knowing that my expression of anger really would not kill anyone as I was taught. Expressing anger was no longer a matter of life or death for me.

A word of caution I learned from a professor in my graduate training. His very first client was a woman who was the victim of physical abuse from her husband. He worked hard to help her learn to assert herself and not keep her anger inward. When she felt strong enough to do so, she confronted her husband with her true feelings, and he beat her so badly she had to be hospitalized. When I suggest expressing your anger outwardly, you need to know your audience. She had changed, but her husband hadn't. In the case of a physical abuser, it is best to get out of the relationship in order to stay safe instead of directing your anger outward to the perpetrator.

Learn to express your anger in appropriate ways. Most importantly, stop turning your anger inward on yourself. You do not deserve to ever be treated that way. Show some compassion for yourself and put the anger where it truly belongs. Do not turn the anger inward on yourself.

Please live!

CHAPTER 78

❖❖❖❖❖

DEATH

The problem with suicide is that it is so final. Once you pull the trigger, or put a noose around your neck, or take the pills, or put into action whatever means you use to end your life, that's it, there is no going back. Death sets into motion a series of un-thought-of painful consequences for the ones you leave behind. The pain spreads like a forest fire leaping from one individual to another until everyone is consumed by your suicide. That may not be your intention but is the outcome others will experience for the rest of their lives.

There was a college student who committed suicide when I worked in the Office of Student Affairs. This student never knew his death would have such a traumatic effect on me and so many others. When I came into work one morning, I heard that one of our students who was a few weeks away from graduating and going on to graduate school, had killed himself. During the pre-dawn hours, he laid on the railroad tracks next to his dormitory on campus and allowed a train to run him over. The Dean of Students called me that morning to ask who lived in a specific room in Brown Hall. The room key was what was being used to identify the body. I was the first person to know who that young man was who ended his life in such a horrific manner. I gave his name to the Dean.

This young man who was alive just hours before was now dead by his own intentions. He would never graduate nor attend graduate school. He would miss out on all that life had to offer him. Nothing good would come from his death, there was no silver lining.

His death was so difficult for so many people. I will never forget his father speaking at the memorial service on campus for his dead son, it was gut-wrenching and still haunts my memories to this day. You never forget tragic moments like this.

I know it was not this student's intention to cause gut-wrenching pain for so many individuals. He was attempting to escape his pain but instead he passed it along to all of us. This is what suicide does. This is the reality no matter what you might be trying to convince yourself otherwise.

Pain passes along as pain, and multiplies as it spreads. The part I want to shout from the rooftops is that it does not have to end like this. This student could have made a much less painful decision because suicide is preventable because depression is treatable.

You can learn from this student. You can make a less painful decision. Depression is treatable. Choose life. Please, I am begging you, in that moment when you are struggling with a decision that is so final to choose life for yourself. Also choose life for all those around you who will most certainly be devastated by your death. Please, choose life.

Please live!

CHAPTER 79

BE AFRAID

If the thought of the process of killing yourself scares you, that is great to hear! Be very afraid. Hold on to that fear. You should be afraid of the process of committing suicide because it is going to be an unnecessary amount of pain you do not have to experience. Killing yourself is not an easy process and is extremely painful. It is also extremely messy and the site of your body remains will be gruesome and leave a lasting horrifying impression on any individuals who have to witness and remove your dead body. Whatever method you have thought about using to destroy yourself, please think again about that process and the aftermath.

I used to think I could slice my wrists and bleed to death, but cutting was much more difficult than I had anticipated. I am so thankful now that it was extremely difficult. I also used to fantasize about swallowing a bottle of pills and then peacefully falling into a slumber of unconsciousness that would, in a very few minutes, lead to my death.

The reality was much different for me in my suicide attempt. Instead of drifting off into a peaceful slumber after swallowing a bottle of pills, I ended up in an emergency room very much awake and scared beyond my ability to cope with the nightmarish reality I created. I recall so vividly the room spinning out of control as I laid on a gurney struggling to understand the questions the emergency staff where asking me. Responding in any accurate manner was nearly impossible. Then quite unexpectedly, projectile vomit began spewing from my mouth and went everywhere. I remember being surprised by how violent the vomiting was and how bad it smelled to the point of making it difficult to breathe. A nurse began pouring liquid charcoal down my throat. There was nothing peaceful about this experience. Be afraid.

Years later, there was a patient at a psychiatric hospital I worked at that had shot himself in the face in a suicide attempt. To his surprise, and everyone else's, he survived the gunshot wound to his face. Now he still had to solve the problem that brought him to this place where he thought suicide was going to be his best plan of action. And, in addition to his depression, he had to deal with his disfigured face. It was difficult for me to look at him, especially knowing he had done this to himself. Not in a judgmental way like shame on him but in a compassionate way where I wished he had been too afraid to pull the trigger.

My husband knew an individual from work who hung himself. He succeeded but not in the manner he had planned. He had placed a noose around his neck and stood on a chair expecting to kick the chair out from under his legs which he assumed would snap his neck and kill him instantly. Instead, he strangled to death struggling over the next several hours to loosen the noose around his neck while desperately stretching his legs out to reach the knocked over chair below him. Sadly no one found him in time to save his life.

Be afraid. Do not have faith in fantasies that suicide holds a peaceful way out of your problems. It does not. Reality and fantasy could not be any further apart as they are on this issue. If you think it takes courage to kill yourself, use that same courage to live another day. Living takes courage. Be afraid to commit suicide. I guarantee there will come a day that you will be so thankful you were too afraid to go through on any suicidal plan. Please be afraid! Please let me scare you enough with the truth of committing suicide that you find the will to live another day.

Please live!

CHAPTER 80

SOLUTIONS

Do not kill yourself while you are experiencing an emotional storm because like all storms, it will pass. The problems you are experiencing are similar to the fear you feel when you are caught outside during a severe thunderstorm. Blinding rain, thunder, lightning, and high winds can be terrifying to experience. As scary as these times are when storms feel all powerful and life-threatening, they will pass. There is nowhere on Earth where it storms continually. The same can be said in life, there is no problem that will last forever without a solution.

There are no problems worth killing yourself over. None. No matter how serious the problems may be, they do not warrant a death sentence. There is nothing you can do wrong that would ever be worth taking your life. Nothing!

Even if you did do something terribly wrong, suicide is not the answer. Taking responsibility for your actions and making amends is a much better solution. Your death will not produce the forgiveness you need, but finding a way to right the wrong by putting into action some form of restitution will help ease the consequences. Everyone has the power to turn their life around if they choose to do so.

You do not have to die. Suicide will not resolve the problem, but only create more chaos. What you must focus on is finding solutions to your problems so they can end once and for all. Whatever your problem is, there is a solution. This is where counseling with a mental health professional can be life-changing. Exploring ideas for solutions to your problems can open up your world in ways you were unable to see or even imagine prior to counseling.

Solutions take action. Have the courage to know you have the power to solve your problems. Believe in yourself. Know that I believe in your power to solve your problems without committing suicide. Know I believe in you and your abilities to be a problem solver. Seek solutions. No matter how difficult it may be to turn and face your problems head on, the sheer satisfaction of getting to a better place is the reward you will receive for all your efforts. Do not let suicide be your solution. Always choose life as your first solution to your problems. From there, the rest of the solutions you require will come with time. I promise you they will!

Remember this, when you are actively suicidal, you are experiencing an emotional storm that will pass. Please in that moment, choose life and seek mental health treatment. The storm will pass and you need to be alive so you can once again enjoy the warmth of the sun and the blue skies that always follow the storm.

Please live!

CHAPTER 81

FORGIVE YOURSELF

If you have made mistakes, you really need to find a way to forgive yourself. We are not born to be perfect. Perfection is not part of our DNA. We are created not to be perfect; but rather to be human. That is why forgiveness is such a great gift we can offer ourselves when things go wrong because of poor decisions we have made along the way.

Every time we wake up from a night's rest we have an opportunity to live a new day. We do not have to bring our mistakes with us into this new day. We can leave them in the past, having learned from them what we needed to learn. Mistakes can be a gift if we bring from them something that helps us live a better life.

Forgiving yourself may not be easy, but it is important. Some of us are so accustomed to punishing ourselves because we feel guilty. But what if that were not the case? Instead, what if we made a mistake and learned a painful lesson from that mistake? What if that mistake taught us never to do that again? Then the mistake has had a purpose, and our life improves. So always do your best, forgive yourself when you need to, and move forward with your life.

I made a huge mistake. I allowed an individual that I believed loved me, to treat me in ways I should never have allowed. The consequences were devastating. It took me a long time to understand I deserved to be treated better. I realized I deserved forgiveness from myself for this mistake because I had suffered enough. Once I learned that lesson, I was able to set boundaries in future relationships so no one would ever treat me like that again. My life became something to celebrate all because I learned from a mistake.

It took me a long time to get to a better place. What I would like to suggest is that you begin to practice forgiving yourself with small mistakes you make. Then perhaps you can begin working on forgiving yourself for the more difficult mistakes. We beat ourselves up way too much. So start with something small, for instance the next time you forget to pick something up at the store, instead of beating yourself up about it, smile at your forgetfulness and go back to the store and pick up what you did not purchase; problem resolved. If there was a time when you left home and you weren't sure whether you locked the door and you had to go back to check, smile at yourself knowing that all is well and the problem is now resolved. Perhaps you left a window open and it rained in on your floor. Instead of beating yourself up once again, dry everything off and be happy that your problem is resolved with the added advantage of now having a clean and shiny floor.

By smiling at yourself or even laughing at your mistake, you are learning to develop compassion for yourself. You deserve compassion. Everyone deserves compassion. The more you practice not taking your small mishaps so seriously, the more you will be able to tackle the bigger mistakes.

Do you know the funniest comedians are those who tell the audience jokes about the mistakes they made in life? They make the audience laugh so hard because they see themselves making the same mistakes. When people open up and are vulnerable with their stories of hardships and mistakes, we feel most connected to them because they have an understanding about not being perfect all the time. The comedians allow us to share in their imperfections that we can relate to.

Laughing at your mistakes can be life-saving. Finding empathy and compassion for yourself is a gift you deserve to receive. Guilt is a wasted emotion, so do not invite guilt into your life. Instead, invite laughter into your life. It is okay to make mistakes. It is okay to forgive yourself. No matter what you have done or think you have done, always choose forgiveness. Choose your life.

Please live!

CHAPTER 82

＋◆◆◆◆＋

PLAY FOR FUN

In order to relax and live a more stressed free and happy life, you need to find ways to play for fun. This is so important because we are here on this earth now and we need to take advantage of all that life has to offer us in this moment. So how do you discover this way of being that captures the essence of the happiness you so desperately seek? I discovered a piece of happiness that I will hold onto forever.

Now that I am retired, I decided to take piano lessons. I was lucky to find a wonderful piano teacher in Las Vegas! His name is, Robert Anthony, and he is an accomplished musician. He is training me to be a musician as well, instead of just a piano player. He expands my mind with every lesson. I love our time together talking and playing music.

One music lesson, I mentioned to Robert that I was going on vacation and would not be able to practice on the piano for several weeks. Robert suggested I take the time I had available on the piano before our next lesson and "play for fun."

I complied with his instructions because I value his opinion and I spent the time I had available playing the piano for fun. What a difference. I was accustomed to sitting down at the piano and working on my scales and finger exercises. I worked at reading music. I worked at learning new songs. Now, I had permission from Robert, my mentor, to play for fun. I loved every second playing the piano with that particular focus. My playing sounded so much better to me because having fun was my goal.

I began to realize that I play the piano the same way I live life. I take life so seriously. I work at it constantly. I painstakingly give it my best. And then came, "play for fun." Really, I get to play for fun in life? I can make life fun and that's okay? That thought made me laugh.

At my next piano lesson, I told Robert how much I enjoyed playing for fun, and how doing so had greatly increased the amount of enjoyment I experienced. Hearing me, he literally assigned "play for fun" on my list of what to work on for the following two weeks. I would be sure to follow his instructions from that point forward every time I sat down at the piano to play.

So, let me instruct you with Robert Anthony's wise words if I may, "play for fun." Whatever you have to do, do it with playfulness. Enjoy the tasks at hand. Find ways to make work playful. Be silly. Be creative. Be whatever makes the time pleasurable for you. Do whatever you are doing that makes your heart sing.

Please lighten up and do not take life so seriously. Play for fun!

Please live!

CHAPTER 83

LAUGHTER

There is a secret to happiness that every two-year old knows, but is unable to verbalize in language form yet, and that secret is laughter. We have two, two-year old granddaughters and all they want to do is laugh and make others laugh. Our one, two-year old granddaughter, goes around the house saying, "I'm funny!" She's right, she is funny. Both of the girls are funny because laughing is what they love to do. Their focus in life is so simple and so fun.

I'm guessing that you have not participated in much laughter lately. It is hard to laugh when you are feeling depressed. Laughter can be an important key to feeling better, if only for a moment. Look around for something to laugh about. I usually start with myself. I am always doing something that makes me laugh at myself. In those moments when I am able to not take myself so seriously, and I do something goofy, I let myself laugh. For instance, I left the house to go shopping the other day and it wasn't until I was exiting my vehicle that I realizing I was still wearing my big fluffy slippers and that made me laugh. I live for those moments.

Here is an idea, look for something funny every day and write it down. Start a Laughter Journal. Here is where you get to do some "work" in order to feel better. What do you find funny? You don't have to write a book, just jot something down. The act of looking for something funny to write in your Laughter Journal will help you focus your attention on funny things throughout your day.

Our granddaughters laugh at the swirling Mickey Mouse lights we have on our ceiling in our family room. They laugh when they jump and dance around the room. They laugh when they chase each other from room to room while they giggle so hard it makes us laugh with them. What is really amazing to witness is when they trip and fall down, they look around and get up laughing, then continue on with their play. What a gift that they can make a mistake and laugh about it. They take every opportunity to laugh just for laughter's sake.

If you can't find laughter in your life, then at least smile. The act of smiling releases endorphins in the brain, the feel good chemicals. Keep smiling until you can enjoy some form of laughter from some moment in your day. If all else fails, google "baby laughing" on the computer and watch a real champ do it.

Please live!

CHAPTER 84

GOOD ENOUGH

Good enough is a measure we use to judge ourselves and more often than not it tends to be a harsh judgment. So many of us lack the confidence needed to see ourselves in a positive light and thus beat ourselves up for not being good enough. We suffer needlessly when we hold the belief that we are not good enough, when in reality, that is not true.

I had always believed I was not good enough. I did not excel at anything in particular growing up. I was not an athlete. I was not a cheerleader. I was not a Homecoming Queen. I was not an "A" student. I did not have a solo voice. I was not even very good at playing a musical instrument. In truth, I was looking at this all wrong and misjudging myself. It wasn't that I was not good enough, it was that my lack of confidence in my abilities shrouded my thinking to the point where I could not see my own value and worth.

It is so painful to believe you are not good enough. Being 'not good enough' becomes a judgement call. Who is telling you that you are not good enough? The important lesson here is that you are actually amazing. You just need to discover what activities make you feel amazing. When I was growing up, I tried playing sports but in truth I never liked the idea of competition. I prefer situations that do not pit one person against another. I know other people thrive on competition and I respect them for that because I can see how it works in their lives by giving them a sense of drive to accomplish great feats. You have to figure out what works best for you and then follow your own way of being in the world; learning and putting into practice your own standards. For instance, when I golf with my husband and sons, I do not keep my score. That way golfing with them is fun and makes me happy. I will never be good enough by the Ladies' Professional Golf Association (LPGA) standards, but I am good enough by my standards.

I love music and am currently taking piano lessons. I am not good enough to perform for others outside my home, but that is okay with me because I play the piano for my own entertainment and the enjoyment of my husband and granddaughters who dance around the living room as I play for them. Thus my piano playing is good enough.

I am not a writer, but I have published several books about overcoming adversities and learning how to love myself so that others can do the same. I know with certainty that I will never win the Pulitzer Prize, but that's okay. My purpose in writing is always to help myself and hopefully give others insight into their lives so they too will be able to reach their full potential. If this book helps even one individual choose life instead of death, then my writing is good enough.

Deciding whether or not you are good enough is a judgment call you do to yourself. Find ways to enjoy the parts of your life where you make activities be what you enjoy them to be. Do not keep score if you don't want to, play for fun, or write your story. You are good enough. You have always been good enough. You will always be good enough. Believe in yourself like I believe in you.

Please live!

CHAPTER 85

+ ✦✦✦✦✦ +

THE SEDUCTION OF SUICIDE

In Homer's *The Odyssey* the main character Odysseus was warned about the Sirens. These were creatures that sang seductively with the purpose of luring sailors to commit suicide by sailing their ships into rocks, resulting in sinking their ships and drowning. Odysseus was determined to hear the Sirens but devised a plan to keep himself and his crew alive. The only way Odysseus made it past the Sirens safely was to put earwax in all the crews' ears so they would not be able to hear the singing and then have the crew tie him to the mast so he could not jump overboard to swim toward the Siren's beautiful seductive music and drown. Taking these necessary precautions ahead of time saved everyone onboard. Suicide is seductive like the Sirens' songs. Suicide has a luring quality about it, a fantasy that promises relief from the emotional pain and problems of this world. Like Odysseus, you must take precautions ahead of time against this fantasy of a seductive death in order to survive.

Death is no fantasy. Death is final.

There is nothing beautiful about the reality of death by suicide. Committing suicide is an ugly affair. Suicide is violent no matter what fantasy you choose to believe in regarding how it will happen. Be assured none of that is true. A gun shot is painful, violent, and bloody. Taking pills is violent to your inner organs that results in vomiting and possible seizures. Cutting yourself is painful, violent, and again bloody. Hanging yourself is also painful, violent, and grotesque. For the individuals that discover your body, and also for the people who have to clean up the scene after your death, your suicide is a gruesome image that will haunt them for the rest of their lives. There is no peaceful ending with suicide, only severe pain, violence, and horror.

I once knew a neighbor whose husband committed suicide by hanging. Unfortunately, she was the first person to discover his body. Her biggest regret in life was that in her panicked state, she called 911 first and then her daughter. Her daughter came over to the house immediately to be with her and witnessed her father's body hanging there in such a grotesque manner. This was an image she blamed herself for ever having shared with her daughter. No matter how any of us attempted to ease her pain around having made the decision to call her daughter in that moment of shock, we all knew she would never forgive herself.

Do not be lured by a fantasy of suicide. Do what you need to do to see suicide in a realistic light. See suicide as a violent death not as a fantasy where you look like you are sleeping peacefully. With suicide you create and accept a gruesome death. And, the gruesome death you create, realistically becomes a horrific nightmare for all those individuals who ever loved or knew you.

See the reality of suicide. Do not be lured by the fantasy like that of the Sirens of Homer. Take life-saving precautions ahead of time as Odysseus did by blocking your ears or tying yourself to the mast of life and holding on. Please survive.

Please live!

CHAPTER 86

＋＊＋＊＋＊＋＊＋＊＋

YOUR ENVIRONMENT

You have complete control of your surroundings so create an environment you love. I love Christmas trees. I take the time to put up five Christmas trees during the holiday season because I enjoy picking each ornament out of its box, unwrapping it from its tissue paper, marveling at its beauty and the memories it brings, then hanging it on the tree and watching the beauty of the tree grow. I have a lifetime of ornaments on our trees. Some ornaments have become so fragile with time, having been made out of construction paper when my children were in kindergarten. Some ornaments were gifts from family members and friends; even from friends who have passed away. Some ornaments are from places I have visited. Each ornament represents a memory for me, so I treasure each and every one of them and the sheer joy they bring to me every holiday season.

At the end of one Christmas season, it occurred to me, how sad it made me to wrap each ornament in tissue paper then put them away for another ten months. So instead, I decided to keep my favorite ornaments on one tree and keep that tree up all year-round. We now have one full size tree in our hallway by our front door. I keep forgetting that everyone does not keep a Christmas tree up all year because ours has become such a part of our home. It is only when someone new comes to visit and is surprised by a Christmas tree displayed during the summer that I realize what we do is so different. When asked why we do this we say it brings joy and happiness to our lives as we are reminded of good times and people that we love.

You too can be different in the sense that you can create whatever kind of environment that makes you happy. You can decorate your home with something that makes you smile every time you notice it. You do not have to follow anyone else's ideas of what your home should or should not look like. There is a sense of freedom that comes with being able to choose how you want your surroundings to look. What appeals to you?

Paint a room or one wall a color that delights you. Frame a picture that represents something you adore in this world. Surround yourself with items that hold beauty for you. Surround yourself with items that hold fond memories for you.

Get rid of items in your environment that do not represent your heart. You do not have to hold on to things that do not bring you joy when you look at them. Just because your parents did something a certain way does not obligate you to do the same or have the same things if they do not delight your soul.

Get organized by clearing out the clutter in your environment so you can make room for what you want in your life. The more organized your items are the more organized your entire life will be. You have complete control over your home's environment. Create your environment so you have a place in the world where you can truly relax and feel content. Create a space that when you look around, you see the world from a happy place. My friends know my home is my sanctuary, my place of refuge and safety. I always want my home to be my happy place. Create an environment all your own. Create your happy place.

Please live!

CHAPTER 87

YOU ARE A TREASURE

You are a treasure! I know this to be true because we are all treasures. Humans are amazing creatures! Your mind is amazing! Your body is amazing! Your heart and ability to love is amazing! Your development from infant to adulthood is amazing! You get into trouble when you start taking yourself for granted and stop appreciating the treasure you truly are.

Take time to appreciate your mind. You have learned to do so much. You can create. You can think your way out of problems, or better yet, you can let your mind be still and find the peacefulness behind your thoughts. You have the power to focus your thoughts on what is happy and healthy for you. You have the power to create a life you love by using your thoughts to make it happen.

Take time to appreciate your body. Did you know you have twenty-seven bones in each hand? Did you know your eyes have three types of color-sensitive cones? Did you know the tears you cry when you are sad are different than the tears you cry when you stub your toe? Did you know that your heart pumps blood to itself first before it pumps blood to the other organs in your body? Have you ever had the ability to watch an Echocardiogram performed and watch the valves of a heart open and close? It is an astonishing procedure to witness. Begin a love affair with your body by acknowledging all of its integral parts that allow you to function so incredibly.

Speaking of the heart, take time to appreciate your ability to love and be loved. Matters of the heart impact every other part of your being.

When the relationship with yourself or others go well, you have energy to spare. No matter what happens, you deserve an abundant happy life. Keep your heart open to giving and receiving love.

Learn to love yourself and appreciate your mind, body, and heart. Take time to thank your feet for taking you where you are going. Thank your mind the next time you solve a problem. Thank your heart when you show love to another human being. See yourself as the treasure that you truly are and give yourself the respect you so deserve.

Please live!

CHAPTER 88

$\diamond\diamond\diamond\diamond\diamond\diamond\diamond$

LABELS

Labels we give each other can be damaging or they can be empowering. Were you the problem child or the trophy child in your family? Which child do you think enters adulthood with confidence? Which child would you rather be? Labels matter. Do not accept what others say about you, not even if they are only joking. If the label they give you is not empowering, see that as a fault of theirs, not yours.

"Scatter Brain" was a song my parents listened to while we were growing up. They decided it was one of my sisters' theme song. The words to the song, much like the title were not flattering. For instance, part of the lyrics were, "…isn't it a pity that you're such a scatter brain. When you smile it's so delightful, when you talk it's so insane, still it's charming chatter, scatter brain." This scatter brain label was not meant to harm my sister, it was all in fun. But fun for who? Not for her.

We had a Sisters Week recently where all three of my sisters and I spent a week together, often reminiscing about growing up. There are twelve years between my oldest sister and me, I being the youngest sister. Our scatter brain labeled sister looked up the song on You-Tube so she could play it for us. She told us, now fifty-five years later, how negatively that song had affected her. It hurt her to think my parents did not value her intelligence. She was not an "A" student in grade school when this record played in our house. I always believed her grades reflected all the moves from one school to another that she had to endure because our father kept changing jobs. Later in life, she went to college and under circumstances that were more conducive to learning, she discovered she was an "A" student.

In the workplace my husband, Andy, had a variety of nicknames given to him by co-workers over the years. The one he loves to this day is, "Android" or "Droid" for short. This label was empowering for him and spoke to his logical thinking. Toward the end of his career, one manager began calling him "Ann," instead of "Andy," in an attempt to demoralize him. In an effort to squash this manager's harassment, Andy started using "Ann." He even changed his first name in emails. When he answered the phone he would say, "Ann speaking." He played with the label so it became his joke, rather than an attack on his masculinity. Inadvertently, Andy beat this manager at his own game by not accepting the label as the manager had intended. When upper management discovered what this manager had attempted to do to Andy, they demanded that he stop his abuse of power. When you receive a label you do not appreciate, let it go, or make it your own so it loses its power to hurt you.

Just as important, watch for the labels you give yourself. Make sure that what you say about yourself is kind. How different would your life be if you told yourself how talented, loving, courageous, bold and strong you are? Do you use words like that to describe yourself? Why not? What label would you give yourself that is empowering? Make this word your mantra. Say it to yourself until it becomes a part of you. Focus on being more generous with praise for yourself. Be proud of yourself for making it through to this day. This is a real accomplishment because life is not always easy to navigate. But life is worth living.

Please remember to be kind and empowering when you choose to label yourself.

Please live!

CHAPTER 89

◆ ◆ ◆ ◆ ◆ ◆ ◆

SELF-NURTURER

If your childhood was not particularly pleasant because you did not have adults in your life that were nurturing, give yourself now, what you did not receive from them in your past. Take care of yourself now the way you wish they would have taken care of you. One difficult aspect of childhood is that, as a child, you had very little control, if any, over your environment. One outstanding aspect of adulthood is you now have total control of how you treat yourself.

Be a self-nurturer. You have the right to give yourself the respect, compassion, caring, dignity, and unconditional love that every human being deserves. What does respect for yourself look like to you? What does compassion for yourself look like? What does it mean to be caring to yourself? What does your dignity look like? How does unconditional love for yourself show up in your life? How can you incorporate these aspects into your daily routine?

The opposite of these nurturing aspects are cruelty, abusiveness, and neglect. Are these part of your life? If so, how do these show up in your life? How are you cruel to yourself? How are you abusive to yourself? How are you neglectful to yourself?

Sometimes when children grow up with cruelty, abusiveness, and neglect from the adults who were supposed to love them, they believe they deserve to be treated that way in adulthood. In childhood, you did not have a choice because you did not have the control. As an adult, you choose how you treat yourself as well as how you allow others to treat you.

Choose nurturing skills for yourself. Choose unconditional love for yourself. Expect to be treated well and do not tolerate relationships where you are not nurtured and respected. Be kind to yourself. Create for yourself what you did not receive. Be a self-nurturer.

Please live!

CHAPTER 90

✦✦✦✦✦✦

HATERS

Do not give up because of Haters. Do not let Haters win by killing what is good in this world for you. Haters are people who go out of their way to make others as miserable as they are. They do not care who they hurt or what consequences come from their cruelty.

I know a musician who stopped performing because he was so discouraged having to deal with criticism from people who do not play a musical instrument nor perform in any capacity. In truth, this individual is a phenomenal musician by anyone's standards. What makes this so sad is that the world desperately needs more artists, like this musician, to take us to places with their music that provide moments of pure bliss. Haters kill bliss. Haters do not want others to be happy.

One way to counter this is to not take the criticism personally. Haters do not care about your feelings or anyone else's. You do not matter to them. No one matters to them. What you have to do is find a way to manage the criticism for what it is. The criticism coming from Haters has no truth nor value. Haters focus on anyone crossing their path. Their criticism will be directed at any individual who happens to be within their reach; it's not personal to you. This is their problem.

By believing in the criticism that is directed your way by a Hater, you give that person power over you when you put any validity to what they are saying. Keep your power by knowing the truth of what you believe in and what is good for you. The more you re-play their cruel words in your thoughts, the more power they gain to hurt you.

One way to put a Hater in perspective is to see this person in a whole new light. A great example of this came from a McDonald's Happy Meal that included a little red stuffed dragon toy the day before my divorce hearing. This little red stuffed dragon, with its angry face, reminded me a great deal of my soon to be ex-husband. I had seen his angry face intentionally intimidating me way too many times but it was about to end. It was empowering for me to have this little red dragon with me in court as a reminder that my ex-husband had no more control over me than did this angry looking little toy.

See Haters for what they are. They spew cruel words but you choose whether you give those words power. See these words as nothing more than a television show you can turn off. Take back your power from Haters.

Please live!

CHAPTER 91

✦ ◆◆◆ ✦

GRIEF

"**I**f you jump, I jump," I told my husband, Andy, early on in our relationship. What I meant by this is, if he were to die before me, I would die soon after. I could not fathom what it would be like to exist in this world without him by my side. He inhales and I exhale.

If you are feeling suicidal due to having lost a loved one, my heartfelt condolences are with you. The depth of grief one feels for those they have loved and lost is extremely difficult to endure. At the age of sixteen, I remember how strange it was when my father died, and the world did not stop because of his death. I felt as though it should have stopped but life went on.

As difficult as this time in your life may be, you cannot give up. Even if your soulmate and best friend has died, you must live. Andy tells me frequently that if he dies first, it is my responsibility to carry on our legacy. I must, he insists, do the activities we love doing together to remember him. He suggests, "Go play golf for us, spend time with our grandchildren and talk about our times together, go for a walk in our favorite park, or go to the casino and play several of my favorite slot machines for me." Then once a year, on his birthday, Andy wants our family and friends to gather together to remember him by having a BBQ and grilling up hamburgers made from his special recipe (half ground meat, half Bob Evans sausage, mixed with honey and BBQ sauce) along with drinking a beer or two in his honor. Andy wants to know that his zest for life will continue even after his death.

My sister-in-law, who lost our brother to kidney cancer when they were both forty-one years old, tells us that Hensman (my maiden name) women are strong. My oldest sister lost her husband several years ago to a sudden heart attack. Another one of my brother-in-law's died last year from multiple myeloma. My two sisters and sister-in-law have all shown a great deal of strength as they go through this grieving process. I have an enormous amount of admiration for their coping abilities. I know they have been a great support system for each other and I have learned so much from witnessing their compassion, endurance, and concern for one another.

If you are grieving the loss of a loved one, honor them by continuing their legacy. Honor them in ways that bring you comfort. Do not give up on life. Keep their heart alive within your beating heart. Different individuals come in and out of our lives. Turn your attention to the living. Love the ones around you that still grace this earth. Create your own support system. Also, consider joining a grief support group if that would be helpful. The folks who run grief support groups are such caring and understanding people. Plus being around people who have also experienced the loss of a loved one will help you cope with your new situation.

I was wrong to say if Andy jumped, I would jump. I said that out of fear. I have learned over these past fifteen years we have been together how important we both are. Both of our hearts are necessary here. It is our responsibility and honor to continue on with life even if one of us has to leave a little sooner than the other. I also take heart in the wise words spoken by the Grandmother in the Disney movie *Moana*, "There is nowhere you could go that I would not be with you." Love never dies.

Please live!

CHAPTER 92

✦✦✦✦✦

LIFE AFTER SUICIDE

Many people have strong beliefs about the afterlife. If you are seriously contemplating suicide because you believe that will put an end to all your problems, please ask yourself this question, what do you believe will happen to you after your death? Just for a moment, suppose your existence after death continues on in spirit form. And what if in this new life your problems continue and you no longer have the ability to control or escape from this existence? Suicide is not possible because your body is already dead and you cannot kill your spirit. Hell would not be a place of fire and brimstone, but rather it could be an existence where you see what your life would have been knowing you can no longer live that life. This would be tragic. This would be sad. So the real question becomes, assuming that no one really knows what happens after death, is it the end or is it just the beginning? With that in mind, why choose the unknown when you don't have to?

Right now, you have the power to choose to live your life. You already have what you need most in life, which is happiness, peace, and love within your spirit. You just need to find ways to look into your inner resources and tap into those positive energies. Quiet your mind by learning to meditate and discover your inner peace. That is when you will hear the small voice within you telling you what you need to do to stay alive.

When you picture yourself taking your last breath in this world, don't you want to envision yourself going into your next existence with the peace of mind that comes from having lived a full and happy life?

Don't rob yourself of time. Don't take your last breath regretting the fact that you ended your life too soon without living the full life that was given to you. You want your final thoughts to be ones where you have an opportunity to look back on your life with thankfulness for having been able to love and be loved.

Please do not kill yourself. Remember that suicide is preventable because depression is treatable. You do not have to commit suicide. Do not miss out on your life. Please live the life you so richly deserve and were given to enjoy. Life is a gift not to be taken away by your own hands.

Please live!

CHAPTER 93

◆◆◆◆◆◆

MARTYRDOM

I believe that people misuse martyrdom. Often we see ourselves as virtuous if we are suffering for a good cause or to appear humble. Being truly humble does not mean that we think less of ourselves but rather that we think of others more. First though we must develop a strong sense of our own self-worth. That is not acting selfishly, we need to be in a place of our own power and strength before we can reach out to others. We need to love ourselves first. Loving ourselves does not include suffering.

I come from a long line of martyrs, people who believe in sacrifice and suffering. At an early age, I learned suffering was a virtue, so I became really good at suffering and sacrificing by putting others first even when it was detrimental to me to do so. I attended a Catholic school and from first grade on, I read every saint book in our school library. I wanted to grow up and be just like them. Wanting to be saintly is admirable. However, wanting to be saintly by sacrifice and suffering was definitely taking the wrong approach. Learning to love myself and others would have been a much better way of achieving my childhood goals.

The problem with sacrifice and suffering is that it is demeaning; resulting in the breakdown of an individual's confidence to do anything well. That is not virtuous. Joy is completely nonexistent in this approach. We have not been put on earth to purposely suffer by our own hands. There is already enough built-in suffering that is inherent in being human without creating more. Do you agree?

Shakespeare said it so well throughout Hamlet's Soliloquy "To Be Or Not To Be" when talking about the normal, everyday suffering on earth when he states, "to suffer the slings and arrow of outrageous fortune" or "a sea of troubles" or "the heartache and the thousand natural shocks that flesh is heir to" or "the whips and scorns of time." Life is not always easy. We humans suffer war, poverty, hunger, disease, and the loss of our loved ones and friends that all cause suffering. It is not a virtue to add even more suffering onto yourself by your own actions.

What is important is to look around for ways to help those who are suffering, not create more pain for yourself and others. Please look around to see if there is someone in need you can give assistance to. That will allow you to bring more healing, happiness, and help to other human beings. Show someone you love them; that is a virtue that matters and it will uplift your spirit to do so.

You do not have to sacrifice yourself and suffer for others. Let the martyr in you be replaced with a person who loves and helps others out of their pain. This approach will bring you more joy and contentment in your life. Please do not suffer more than you have to by your own means.

Please live!

CHAPTER 94

RANDOM ACTS OF KINDNESS

How extraordinary would it be today if you choose to do a random act of kindness instead of killing yourself? Instead of something horrific coming from your actions, a grace-filled moment could be the outcome. Please pick something grace-filled over something horrific.

Random acts of kindness are astonishing because of the positive energy they create. That energy not only lives inside the recipient for a moment in time, but also within their memory forever. As life unfolds, the positive energy you put into this world will be reciprocated back to you and enrich your life even more. You feel good when you can do something positive for someone else.

What could you do? How about opening a door for someone? Could you bake cookies for your dentist or doctor and their staffs? Run a 5K race for a good cause? Save your pop tabs for the Ronald McDonald House for sick children and their families? Write someone a poem? Contribute to a charity that holds meaning for you? How about volunteering your time to an organization like the United Way, Red Cross, or your local Veterans Hospital? What about the simple but profound act of smiling and acknowledging someone? I know I always light up when someone smiles at me and says "hello" whether that person is a friend or stranger passing by.

Any random act of kindness is better than planning a way to hurt yourself. Give a random act of kindness to yourself. Do something to treat yourself in a kind, caring fashion.

Please be kind to yourself. Please be kind to others.

Please live!

CHAPTER 95

ROOTING FOR YOU

Besides me, who is rooting for you? Who else wants you to be free of your depressed symptoms so you can live happy with energy to spare? I know this is what I want for you. I know deep down this is what you want for yourself. So far, that makes two of us. Who else in your life, past or present, is rooting for you?

Imagine you have a dinner table and you are going to have dinner with five other people. These five individuals are people who matter most to you. They can be living or deceased. Fill your table by choosing five people who have been supportive, loving, and have valued you. Now that you have five people at your table, six including yourself, visualize how they would counsel you if you shared your honest feelings with them about wanting to commit suicide. What would they say to convince you to stay alive? Go around the table, look each person in the eye, and listen to their concerns for you. Listen to their wisdom and love.

If you can only think of one person in your life that really cared about you, do what I do when I am stressed. I picture myself outdoors in a sunny backyard laying on a hammock in the arms of a person who wants nothing more than to hold me and hear what is troubling me. When I think about it, this person just listens and comforts me. Who would do that for you?

Start thinking about who is rooting for you? Use them to gain strength when you feel depleted. Use them for their concerned wisdom or their quiet comfort.

For fun, you can even fill a stadium of people who are rooting for you. Hear them cheering you on and celebrating the fact that you are alive. Put me in those stands for you because I am rooting for you too.

Gooooo You!!

Please live!

CHAPTER 96

HOPE

"Grounds for believing that something good may happen," is one of the definitions SIRI offers me for the word 'hope' on my Apple iPhone. Give yourself hope. Give yourself the belief that something good will happen for you.

You need to live in order to experience hope. You need to be alive when good things happen for you. There is no bad situation that lasts forever that will rob you of your hope unless you allow it to. When things are not going as you had hoped or expected, you can concentrate on the disaster, or you can look for and concentrate on the silver lining that will bring you comfort.

I won't say all, but most situations have some redeeming value. You have to look for and concentrate on the silver lining of the situation. In a really bad situation, maybe the silver lining is that the negative circumstances have ended. Your future is something to concentrate on and live for.

As long as you hold even a glimmer of hope, you will survive because you will keep looking for a way out of a bad situation. Hope keeps you moving forward. Hope keeps pointing you in the right direction.

If you have lost all hope, there is still hope for you because you are still alive. Keep living until hope returns because hope always returns. People, like myself and many others I know personally, are so thankful our suicide attempts were not successful. We too were once feeling completely hopeless, but now we have found a way out of our hopelessness to a place where good things did happen and we experience peace in our lives.

You need to survive until your life changes for the better. Hold on to the belief that something good will happen for you. Have hope!

Please live!

CHAPTER 97

✦✦✦✦

DREAM

"What do you want to be when you grow up?" Adults ask children this question all the time. It is an adult's way of asking a child to focus on their future. It is not a bad question, it's just that a child does not have the mental capability to understand all the unexpected twists and turns life presents as you age. Their childhood answer will probably not resemble their reality in adulthood.

As an adult, are you where you thought you would be when you used to answer this question? How would you like your life to be? Does this vision of yourself differ from your reality? If so, how would you like to re-set your life so you become what you truly want to be? As long as you are alive, you are able to make changes to your goals and make your dreams come true. For example, you are never stuck in one career because you have the ability to change careers if you so desire.

First, you have to have a dream. If someone asked you today, "What do you want to do with your life," what would your answer be? What if you woke up tomorrow to the perfect world you dream of, what would that dream world look like? So first, you have to have a dream that excites you to take action to make this happen.

Secondly, what big or small action can you take today to begin to move toward your dream? Do you want a different job? Start putting out resumes to jobs that look attractive to you. Never say 'no' for the other person. What this means is to apply to any job that sounds good to you. Do not hold back on applying because you assume the person receiving the resume will reject you. Assume the company wants you until you hear otherwise.

There is a young man that I know who took an English class during his first semester of college. His English professor gave the class an assignment to send out one resume with a cover letter to their dream job. He sent his resume to a video gaming company and actually received an interview followed by a job offer he accepted. Never in a million years would he have thought about sending his resume to this company. It was only following a classroom assignment that resulted in receiving his dream job. Never say "no" for the other person.

Thirdly, if at first you don't succeed, find another route to your dream. One of my dreams was to publish this book. I began putting notes together for ideas in 2012, then I put the notes away. It wasn't until May 12, 2019 that I brought the notes back out of the filing cabinet and began writing these chapters. In 2012, I had difficulty going back and reliving my depression and the suicide of others in order to write about this topic. Now in 2019, time has lessened the emotional pain around these memories and I can write about this subject without the fear of being drawn back into my depression and re-grieving for the loss of family and friends.

Dream. Take action toward the fulfillment of your dreams. Do not give up. Make your dreams come true by exhausting every avenue until you find the pathway to achieve your goals. No matter what, do not stop dreaming.

Do not let your age matter. If you could dream when you were a child, you can still dream now. In fact, as an adult, you have more control to make your dreams come true.

It is fun to dream. Give yourself this opportunity to expand your world in ways that enlighten you. Dream. Dream. Dream. Dream. Dream.

Please live!

CHAPTER 98

A FEW EXTRAS

I have a few more ideas I want to share with you that I hope will deter you from following through on any suicidal thoughts. These are not big ideas that merit an entire chapter, however I do not want to leave any stone unturned in my pursuit to keep you alive. So here are a few more ideas for you to consider.

What about reading an autobiography of someone you admire or are curious about? Often times, autobiographies give us a look into the struggles an individual had to confront and overcome in their lives. Discovering new coping skills that other people used in their lives is always helpful.

How about planting a garden? Giving yourself an opportunity to be outdoors in the fresh air caring for a small garden is a relaxing activity. If you don't happen to have a yard available for a garden, how about purchasing a few potted plants to place in a sunny area of your home? Then, you have the chance to watch your efforts grow and mature. In the end you receive the additional benefit of harvesting and enjoying your very own vegetables, herbs, fruits, or flowers. Does gardening sound like fun to you?

Movies can offer an escape from the here and now. What about watching a movie and relaxing into the drama about someone else's life? How about watching an old movie you love? Obviously this won't solve your depression all by itself; however, it will give you a break from your depressed mood while you are taking steps to have your depression treated.

Have you ever studied poetry? I love it when I find lyrics to a song I can relate to. Recently, I found a song by Bob Dylan that I can't get out of my head, which is great because the words are so profound for me. They definitely speak to my heart. The song is "Make You Feel My Love." If you have never heard this song before, do yourself a favor and listen to it. Go to You-Tube and listen to the words. The words are everything I wish for you. What lyrics to what songs speak to you?

In a moment of despair when ending your life seems like your only option, allow yourself to sleep. Laying down and taking a nap, or going to bed early is a much better decision in that moment than taking steps toward any type of self-harm. If you are exhausted by life and overwhelmed by your present circumstances just try sleeping. Sleep is always better than suicide because you will wake up from sleep and have your life back. Extra rest can help you face your life again with renewed energy.

If your mind is too busy and you cannot sleep, consider writing a bucket list. A bucket list is a term for experiences you want to have before you die. Creating a bucket list is a good idea when you are depressed because it allows your thoughts to focus on a future for you. If money were no object, what would you like to do or see in your lifetime? Picture yourself doing extraordinary things. What would that life look like for you? Create your bucket list. Place it where you are able to see it frequently and keep adding to the list. Better yet, start checking off the activities you actually accomplish that will allow you to find the strength and energy to do even more.

So these are some of my additional ideas that I hope spark even bigger ideas for you. Keep looking for hopeful ways to keep yourself in the game of life.

Please live!

CHAPTER 99

＋◆＋◆＋◆＋

WHAT WILL KEEP YOU ALIVE?

As I am nearing the end of writing this book, I find myself becoming more and more emotional because I care about you! What if I have not written the words you need to hear in order to convince you to keep living?

Instead of me enduring these sad, heartbreaking thoughts for you, it occurred to me to ask you the most important question in the entire book:

WHAT WILL KEEP YOU ALIVE?

What has kept you alive in the past? What do you see keeping you alive in the present moment or future moments? Please take time now and give serious consideration to your answers regarding these questions.

I want to give you the opportunity to write down the words that will keep you alive. Take the rest of this chapter to formulate ideas that would put up a roadblock the next time your thoughts go toward hurting yourself.

No one knows you as well as you know yourself. You know what has kept you from going through with any plan to end your life. What matters most in your life? Use what matters most in your life to create a plan of action to save your life. Please take your time and finish this chapter for me. Write what you need to hear. You are always welcome to share your thoughts on this chapter with me. I would be very interested in knowing what it is that keeps you alive.

Please live!

CHAPTER 100

FINAL THOUGHTS

In the Introduction, I stated, "the goal of this book and all the energy that went into creating it, is to stop your death by suicide by providing other options for you." I want you to live more than I have ever wanted anything in my life. Please help me, in these last few words, help you.

Find your will to live. Right now, place your hand over your heart and feel it beating. There is a reason why you were born with a destiny only you can fulfill. You have a choice and you can choose to ignore your urge to do any type of self-harm. Do not leave the people who love you behind, before your time. A minute of time can seem like an eternity when you are depressed, but the reality is that life goes by so quickly. The more we age, the more we know this to be true.

Suicide is preventable because depression is treatable. Please seek treatment and begin the process of living depressed free, happy, and content. Your heart needs to keep beating so you can achieve your life's full potential. Please keep your heart beating.

I know the urge to kill yourself and end your suffering is an extremely strong emotion but keep my favorite quote in mind. "You are stronger than you know!" Use your strength now to get the help and treatment you need to live without depression.

Take a deep breath. Relax. Go get help. Please fight for yourself. You matter to me. Please fight the depression by seeking treatment. There are trained medical and mental health professionals who want to see you survive, and want to give you the skills to make surviving possible so you can live life to the fullest.

No matter how many times you have tried before, try again. Your focus when you close this book is to live. That's it. Just live!

Thank you for allowing me this great honor of spending this time with you. Please know that I wish you days of sunshine and warmth. I wish you moments of pure joy. I wish you blissful moments. I wish you purpose, meaning, and the ability to reach your full potential. I wish you love and I wish you life!

Please live!

REFERENCES

CHAPTER 2 - CALL THE NATIONAL SUICIDE PREVENTION LIFELINE

1. Howard, J. (2019, June 4). *The US suicide rate is up 33% since 1999, research says.* Retrieved from CNN website; http://www-m.ccn.com.

CHAPTER 3 - DEPRESSION IS TREATABLE

1. Tolentino, J.C., and Schmidt, S.L., (2018, October 2). DSM-5 Criteria and Depression Severity: Implications for Clinical Practice. Retrieved from the National Center for Biotechnology Information, www.ncbi.nlm.nih.gov/pmc/articles/PMC6176119.

CHAPTER 4 - MEDICAL EXAM

1. WebMD. (2018, May 8). Thyroid Symptoms and Solutions. Retrieved from WebMD website, www.webmd.com/women/ss/slideshow-thyroid-symptoms-and-solutions.

CHAPTER 6 - COUNSELING

1. Mueller, D.M. (2009). Sadistic Love: My Twenty-Two Year Marriage To A Sexual Sadist. Bloomington, IN: AuthorHouse.
2. Psychology Today Website. *Find a Therapist.* Retrieved from www.psychologytoday.com on June 27, 2019.

CHAPTER 9 - VITO

1. Wags 4 Warriors is a Nonprofit Organization based in Northeast Ohio. For more information go to www.wags4warriors.org.

CHAPTER 12 - YOU ARE NOT ALONE

1. Whitten, R. (2019, October). Silent Struggles Taboos & Tattoos: Superintendents Are Taking Steps To Save Colleagues Who Contemplate Suicide. Golf Digest.
2. Wan, W. (2019, July 29). *Once they hid their stories. But now survivors of suicide are 'coming out' to combat a national crisis.* www.washingtonpost.com.
3. Quote by Stephanie Sparkles, @SSparlesDaily. mobile.twitter.com. 7:33PM – Feb. 27, 2014.

CHAPTER 20 - BREATHE

1. Hanh, T.N. (1991). Peace Is Every Step. New York, NY: Bantam Books.

CHAPTER 21 - RESILIENCY

1. The Vietnam Veterans Memorial Wall. www.nps.gov/vive/index.htm

CHAPTER 25 - REMOVE DEADLY RISK FACTORS

1. Center for Legislative Archives/National Archives & Records Administration. The Bill of Rights. www.archives.gov.

CHAPTER 27 - THE MAYBE GAME

1. Olya, G. (2018 June 5 @ 6:02PM). Kate Spade's net worth revealed as fashion world loses an icon. www.aol.com.
2. Marcin, T. (2018 June 5 @ 1:14PM). *Kate Spade Net Worth: Massively Successful Designer Dies At 55.* www.newsweek.com.
3. Wikipedia. na. *List of Suicides.* Retrieved May 22, 2019. www.en.m.wikipedia.org.

CHAPTER 28 - DRUGS AND DEPRESSION

1.   Alcoholics Anonymous (AA). www.aa.org.

CHAPTER 30 - LIFE IS ABOUT MAKING GOOD DECISIONS

1.   Frankl, V. (2006). Man's Search For Meaning. Boston, MA: Beacon Press.

CHAPTER 33 - TURN OFF THE TELEVISION

1.   Tolle, E. (2005). A New Earth: Awakening To Your Life's Purpose. New York, NY: Penguin Group.

CHAPTER 34 - FAVORITE BOOKS

1.   Williamson, M. (2010). A Course In Weight Loss. Carlsbad, CA: Hay House, Inc.
2.   Tolle, E. (2005). *A New Earth: Awakening To Your Life's Purpose.* New York, NY: Penguin Group.
3.   Allen, J. (2008). *As A Man Thinketh.* New York, NY: Tarcher/Penguin.
4.   Robbins, A. (1991). *Awaken The Giant Within.* New York, NY: Free Press.
5.   Roth, G. (2010). *Women Food And God.* New York, NY: Scribner.
6.   Brown, B. (2012). *Daring Greatly.* New York, NY: Avery.
7.   Carlson, R. (1997). *Don't Sweat The Small Stuff.* New York, NY: Hyperion.
8.   Hendrix, H. (2008). *Getting The Love You Want.* New York, NY: St. Martin's Press.
9.   Mandela, N. (1995). *Long Walk To Freedom.* New York, NY: Back Bay Books.
10. Frankl, V. (2006). *Man's Search For Meaning.* Boston, MA: Beacon Press.
11. Hahn, T.N. (1991). *Peace Is Every Step.* New York, NY: Bantam Books.

12. Steinem, G. (1992). *Revolution From Within*. Boston, MA: Little, Brown and Company.

13. Lama, D.; Tutu, D.; and Abrams, D. (2016). *The Book Of Joy*. New York, NY: Avery.

14. Ruiz, D.M. (1997). *The Four Agreements*. San Rafael, CA: Amber-Allen Publishing, Inc.

15. Mandino, O. (1985). *The Greatest Salesman In The World*. New York, NY: Bantam Books.

16. Tolle, E. (1999). *The Power Of Now*. Novato, CA: New World Library.

17. Zukav, G. (2014). *The Seat Of The Soul*. New York, NY: Simon & Schuster Paperbacks.

18. Byrne, R. (2006). *The Secret*. New York, NY: Atria Books.

19. Hoff, B. (1982). *The Tao Of Pooh*. New York, NY: E.P. Dutton.

20. Singer, M.A. (2008). *The Untethered Soul: The Journey Beyond Yourself*. Oakland, CA: New Harbinger Publications, Inc.

CHAPTER 35 - VISION BOARD

1. Byrne, R. (2006). The Secret. New York, NY: Atria Books.

2. Red Rock Canyon Marathon, Half Marathon, & 5K. www.calicoracing.com.

CHAPTER 36 - TAKE A HIKE

1. www.movies.disney.com.

CHAPTER 40 - TURN ON THE LIGHTS

1. The Metropolitan Museum of Art. Saint Jerome In a Dark Chamber. Rembrandt. (1642). www.metmuseum.org/art/collection/search/391693.

2. Franciscan Media. na. *Saint Jerome: Saint of the Day for September 30*. *www.franciscanmedia.org*.

CHAPTER 41 – JOIN A GROUP

1. Weight Watchers. www.weightwatchers.com.

CHAPTER 42 – LIVE PERFORMANCE

1. Diana Ross. www.facebook.com>Diana Ross.
2. Cher. www.cher.com.
3. Alice Cooper. www.alicecooper.com.
4. Alanis Morissette. www.alanis.com.
5. Penn & Teller. www.caesars.com/rio-las-vegas.

CHAPTER 43 - RUBBER DUCKIE

1. "Rubber Duckie." The Sesame Street Book and Record. [Recorded by Jim Henson]. Columbia, 1970.

CHAPTER 45 - DECLUTTER

1. Boyles, A. (2018 February 12). 6 Benefits Of An Uncluttered Space. The Psychology Behind Organizing And Decluttering. www. psychologytoday.com.

CHAPTER 46 - 100 ACTIVITIES

1. Bocks, S. (2019). 20 Cheap Date Night Ideas You'll Love. www. thriftyfugalmom.com/cheap-date-night-ideas.
2. Marie Claire Editors, (2019 January 29). *The 40 Best Cheap Date Ideas For Couples On A Budget.* www.marieclaire.com/sex-love/advice/g559/cheap-date-ideas.
3. And Then We Saved. na. (2013 January 21). *Cheap Date Ideas.* www. andthenwesaved.come/cheap-date-ideas.
4. McKay, B. & K. (2016 February 10). *18 At Home Date Ideas.* www. artofmanliness.com/articles/18-At-Home-Date-Ideas.
5. Topp, J. (2011 August 3). *47 Cheap Fun things To Do This Weekend.* www.wisebread.com/47-cheap-fun-things-to-do-this-weekend.

CHAPTER 50 – THE "NO" BUTTON

1. NO Sound Button. Zany Toys LLC, LM-9711.

CHAPTER 55 – SAVE A LIFE

1. Hanna, J. (2017 August 14). Suicides under age 13: One every 5 days. CNN. www.cnn.com/2017/08/14/health/child-suicides/index.html
2. *Suicide in Teens and Children Symptoms & Causes*. na. Boston Children's Hospital. www.childrenshospital.org/conditions...d-teens/symptoms-and-causes.

CHAPTER 57 - CREATE

1. Stern, J.M., & Hulme, M. (Producers), & Stern, J.M. (Director). (2013). Jobs. [Motion Picture]. United States of America: Five Star Feature Films.

CHAPTER 65 – ATTENTION IS A POWERFUL FORCE

1. Mueller, D.M. (2012). 101 Lessons In Love: A Couple's Guide To Choosing Passion. Bloomington, IN: AuthorHouse.

CHAPTER 67 – CHILDHOOD WONDER

1. Proboscis Monkey. www.nationalgeographic.com.

CHAPTER 68 - MUSIC

1. "Alone Again Naturally." [Recorded by Gilbert O'Sullivan]. MAM. 1971.
2. Berms, B., Gad, T., Mendez, L., Jordan, S., & Huff, D. (Producers), *Bridges*. [Recorded by Josh Groban]. United States of America: Reprise.
3. Juggernoud1. (2014). *Piano Selections (Volume 1)*. [Recorded by Noud van Harskamp]. Netherlands. Apple Music.
4. Juggernoud1. (2014). *Beautiful Movie Themes For Piano Solo (Volume 1)*. [Recorded by Noud van Harskamp]. Netherlands. Apple Music.

CHAPTER 71 - GO PLAY

1. Michigan Department of Natural Resources. Master Angler & State Record. www.michigan.gov.

CHAPTER 72 - GENTLY DOWN STREAM

1. "Row Row Row Your Boat." Written by Eliphalet Oram Lyte. Published by The Franklin Square Song Collection. (1881).

CHAPTER 73 - UNDERWHELMED

1. www.thesaurus.com.

CHAPTER 74 – LOWER YOUR EXPECTATIONS

1. "You Can't Always Get What You Want." [Recorded by The Rolling Stones]. Decca (UK), London (US). 1969.

CHAPTER 82 - PLAY FOR FUN

1. Robert Anthony Music. www.robertanthonymusic.com.

CHAPTER 83 - LAUGHTER

1. Disney Magic Holiday Mickey Mouse Whirl-A-Motion LED Projection Spotlight.

CHAPTER 85 - THE SEDUCTION OF SUICIDE

1. Greek Gods and Goddesses. na. (2017 February 7). The Sirens. https://greekgodsandgoddesses.net>myths.

CHAPTER 87 - YOU ARE A TREASURE

1. Wikipedia. na. 27 Bones. www.en.m.wikipedia.org.

CHAPTER 88 - LABELS

1. "Scatter Brain." Freddy Martin and His Orchestra. [Recorded by Freddy Martin and His Orchestra with Vocal by Glen Hughes]. RCA. 1939.

CHAPTER 89 - SELF-NURTURER

1. The Nurturing Parenting Program. na. The Philosophy and Practices of Nurturing Parents.pdf. www.centerforchildrenshealth.org.

CHAPTER 90 - HATERS

1. McDonald's Happy Meal. www.mcdonalds.com.

CHAPTER 91 - GRIEF

1. Shurer, O. (Producer). & Clements, R. & Musker, J. (Directors). (2016). Moana. [Motion Picture]. United States of America: Walt Disney Pictures and Walt Disney Animation Studios.

CHAPTER 93 - MARTYDOM

1. The LitCharts Library. na. Hamlet's Soliloquy, "To Be Or Not To Be" a modern English Translation. www.litcharts.com/blog/shakespeare/hamletssoliloquy. Retrieved date June 28, 2019.

CHAPTER 94 - RANDOM ACTS OF KINDNESS

1. Ronald McDonald House Charities. www.rmhc.org.
2. United Way. www.unitedway.org.
3. Red Cross. www.redcross.org.
4. Veterans Hospital. www.va.gov.

CHAPTER 96 – HOPE

1. Apple iPhone. SIRI. Model: iPhone 7 Plus. Version: iOS 13.1.2. Definition of Hope.

CHAPTER 98 – A FEW EXTRAS

1. "Make You Feel My Love." Time Out of Mind. [Recorded by Bob Dylan]. Columbia. 1997.

ABOUT THE AUTHOR

Deborah M. Mueller holds a Master of Arts in Counseling Degree from Heidelberg University. As a former Licensed Professional Counselor and Owner of Safe Harbor Counseling Center in Anchorville, Michigan, her main area of practice was couples counseling, mood disorders, and grief counseling. She is the author of Sadistic Love and 100 Lessons In Love. In 2015, Deborah retired from counseling and moved to Las Vegas, NV where she continues to write in the hope of lessening the emotional pain for others. She enjoys the warm Las Vegas weather, year-round outdoor activities, and most of all the time spent with her husband, Andy, their children and grandchildren.